Cambridge Elements

Elements in Chinese Economy and Governance
edited by
Luke Qi Zhang
Fudan University
Mingxing Liu
Peking University
Daniel Mattingly
Yale University

TAXATION AND GOVERNANCE IN CONTEMPORARY CHINA

Xiaobo Lü
University of California, Berkeley
Changdong Zhang
Peking University

Shaftesbury Road, Cambridge CB2 8EA, United Kingdom

One Liberty Plaza, 20th Floor, New York, NY 10006, USA

477 Williamstown Road, Port Melbourne, VIC 3207, Australia

314–321, 3rd Floor, Plot 3, Splendor Forum, Jasola District Centre, New Delhi – 110025, India

103 Penang Road, #05–06/07, Visioncrest Commercial, Singapore 238467

Cambridge University Press is part of Cambridge University Press & Assessment, a department of the University of Cambridge.

We share the University's mission to contribute to society through the pursuit of education, learning and research at the highest international levels of excellence.

www.cambridge.org
Information on this title: www.cambridge.org/9781009509725

DOI: 10.1017/9781009509701

© Xiaobo Lü and Changdong Zhang 2025

This publication is in copyright. Subject to statutory exception and to the provisions of relevant collective licensing agreements, no reproduction of any part may take place without the written permission of Cambridge University Press & Assessment.

When citing this work, please include a reference to the DOI 10.1017/9781009509701

First published 2025

A catalogue record for this publication is available from the British Library

ISBN 978-1-009-50972-5 Hardback
ISBN 978-1-009-50969-5 Paperback
ISSN 2976-5625 (online)
ISSN 2976-5617 (print)

Cambridge University Press & Assessment has no responsibility for the persistence or accuracy of URLs for external or third-party internet websites referred to in this publication and does not guarantee that any content on such websites is, or will remain, accurate or appropriate.

For EU product safety concerns, contact us at Calle de José Abascal, 56, 1°, 28003 Madrid, Spain, or email eugpsr@cambridge.org

Taxation and Governance in Contemporary China

Elements in Chinese Economy and Governance

DOI: 10.1017/9781009509701
First published online: December 2025

Xiaobo Lü
University of California, Berkeley

Changdong Zhang
Peking University

Author for correspondence: Xiaobo Lü, xiaobo.lu@berkeley.edu

Abstract: In contrast to the drastic shifts in China's political landscape and society since 2012, taxation may appear as a comparatively mundane topic receiving limited attention. However, the relative stability in China's taxation system underscores its delicate role in maintaining a balance in state–society relations. The Element embarks on an exploration of China's intricate taxation system since the reform era, illuminating its origins and the profound reverberations on state–society relations. It shows that China's reliance on indirect taxation stems from the legacies of transitioning from a planned economy to a market-driven one as well as elaborate fiscal bargaining between the central and local governments. This strategy inadvertently heightens Chinese citizens' sensitivity to direct taxation and engenders the tragedy of the commons, leading to rising government debts and collusion by local governments and businesses that results in land expropriation, labor disputes, and environmental degradation.

Keywords: China, taxation, central–local relations, governance, public opinion

© Xiaobo Lü and Changdong Zhang 2025

ISBNs: 9781009509725 (HB), 9781009509695 (PB), 9781009509701 (OC)
ISSNs: 2976-5625 (online), 2976-5617 (print)

Contents

1 Taxation and State–Society Relations in China – Why Didn't the Dog Bark?   1

2 Lay of the Land: Mapping China's Taxation System and Fiscal Capacity   5

3 Political Logic of Taxation in China   21

4 Taxation and State–Society Relations: Perspectives from Citizens and Business   41

5 Unintended Consequences of Taxation in China   62

6 Final Reflections   75

References   79

1 Taxation and State–Society Relations in China – Why Didn't the Dog Bark?

Budget is the skeleton of the state stripped of all misleading ideologies.

Rudolf Goldscheid

Fiscal capacity is widely regarded as a pillar of the state. Raising fiscal revenue, however, has been and continues to be a highly contentious state–society issue, both historically and contemporarily. After all, the psychology of loss aversion implies that both rich and poor detest relinquishing part of their income to the state as tax payments unless they are necessary, for example, to secure public goods or expand political rights. Failure to resolve implicit or explicit fiscal bargaining erodes state–society relations, inciting mass resentment, social unrest, and eventual tax revolt typically spelling the end of a regime. Fiscal extraction is ubiquitous across states, and authoritarian regimes are no exception because fiscal revenue bolsters their infrastructural power.[1]

Given the centrality of taxation in state–society relations, China remains a puzzling case. By various metrics, the Chinese government has a strong fiscal capacity compared to many countries. Historically, the state's fiscal revenue rarely exceeded 5% of the GDP since the fourteenth century.[2] By 2019, however, the total government revenue amounted to 27.27% of the GDP.[3] Compared to many states – even China before the founding of the People's Republic in 1949 – the state's strong fiscal capacity has encountered relatively little resistance because the government seldom resorts to blunt coercion for most tax collection. Taxation is rarely the primary cause of social unrest in contemporary China.[4] Even when taxation was a key source of conflict sparking rural unrest in the 1990s, agricultural taxes amounted to less than 6% of the total government fiscal revenue.

Paradoxically, the Chinese government has undertaken several tax cut reforms despite local governments face mounting fiscal pressure and looming government debt.[5] Take personal income tax (PIT) as an example: Since the 1980s, both the share of PIT in government revenue and the pool of taxpayers have steadily increased, driven by China's booming economy. This is an ideal

---

[1] Slater and Fenner (2011) identify four mechanisms: funding coercive apparatus to control rivals, strengthening extractive capacity to withstand crises, enhancing state legibility through information collection, and fostering dependence via patronage and clientelism.
[2] See Wang (2022) for historical taxation as a share of GDP in China from 1000 to 1900.
[3] If we use the broadest definition of government revenue, the total revenue as percent of GDP could reach 35%. See Figure 3.3 and discussion in Section 2 for more details.
[4] See discussion in Ong and Göbel (2014).
[5] For the origins and consequences of Chinese government debts, especially those of local governments, see Liu, Oi, and Zhang (2022). For the risks in China's financial system, see Song and Xiong (2018).

scenario in which the government retains greater revenue from PIT without having to raise the tax rate; nonetheless, the Chinese Government has repeatedly raised the exemption threshold for PIT since 2006, along with some adjustments of marginal tax rates. Effectively, these reforms shrank the tax base for PIT and reduced its contribution to total government tax revenue. In addition, the share of taxes on goods and services declined from close to 60% of total tax revenue in 1999 to barely 40% by 2021.

The apparent low political salience of taxation among ordinary citizens and businesses, coupled with the Chinese government's repeated tax cut initiatives, defies conventional wisdom. The spatial models of electoral competition posit that tax policies are driven by the "median voter" and redistributive preferences (Esping-Andersen 1990; Meltzer and Richard 1981; Steinmo 1993). In China, by contrast, policymaking is driven by elite politics and central–local government bargaining, not by the aggregation of mass preference through elections. Although policymaking in autocracies could respond to the need to appease the public, the low salience of tax grievance implies that the government did not initiate these tax cuts to mitigate social unrest in China – except perhaps in the case of the abolition of agricultural taxes in 2006.

Meanwhile, special interest groups, particularly business elites, are crucial players who exert enormous influence on tax policymaking in both democracies and nondemocracies (Dixit, Grossman, and Helpman 1997; Fairfield 2015; Martin 1991; Winters 2011). The Chinese Communist Party (CCP) has meticulously undermined the ability of any organization to overcome the collective action problem in the political sphere. Hence, these tax reforms rarely resulted from any intense lobbying and pressures from economic elites. Finally, major tax reforms are often sparked by exogenous shocks like the global financial crisis and international tax competition (Basinger and Hallerberg 2004; Hays 2011; Swank 1998; Wallerstein and Przeworski 1995). These Chinese tax reforms, except for the 2008 value-added tax (VAT) reform, met with no external pressures.

To shed light on this perplexing development of taxation and state–society relations in China, we investigate three crucial questions in this Element. First, what objectives does the Chinese government seek to accomplish through its tax policies? Second, why hasn't taxation emerged as a prominent issue motivating Chinese citizens and businesses to politically engage with the government? Last, what are the unintended consequences stemming from the Chinese government's strategy in taxation?

We delve into the logic of taxation from the perspective of the Chinese government, contending that tax policies have been an important instrument for the Chinese central government to serve three policy goals: Raising fiscal revenues, stimulating economic development, and maintaining political stability.

These objectives, however, engender a trilemma, forcing the Chinese central government to balance tradeoffs by prioritizing one goal over the others. Crucially, the central government's policy implementation relies on local governments, which frequently exercise their discretionary power to selectively fulfill competing mandates from higher-level authorities. In response, the central government initiates tax reforms to address the challenges resulting from the trilemma, inadvertently creating further unintended consequences, and thus requiring subsequent adjustments.

Second, we contend that the low saliency of taxation in Chinese society is by design. During the Maoist era, the socialist economic model rendered direct taxation unnecessary because the state controlled nearly all aspects of economic production and distribution. When China transitioned to a market-oriented economy after 1978, the state prioritized taxes on goods and services, targeting firms, not individuals, as the primary tax base. Consequently, business taxes account for more than 90% of total government tax revenues to date. Despite shouldering most of the tax burden, Chinese businesses have not actively engaged in politics to push for policy changes. Instead, they adopt atomized strategies to reduce their tax burdens through legal or illegal means and seek preferential policy treatments via political connections. Furthermore, the reliance of indirect taxation on China's tax structure implies that Chinese businesses could shift a large portion of their nominal tax burden to downstream businesses and consumers, mitigating their perceived tax burden.

Third, we contend that the Chinese government's efforts to diminish the saliency of taxation in state–society relations inadvertently generate new sources of tension. Specifically, advocating for lightening the tax burden on citizens amplifies their sensitivity to potential tax increases in the future, largely because of citizens' unrealistic expectations resulting from the state's continuous promise of low taxes. This dynamic constrains the state's ability to extract taxes from alternative sources, perpetuating a cycle of continual tax reductions. Meanwhile, local governments face immense pressure to raise fiscal revenue while promoting economic growth and financing local public goods. This has led to escalating government debt and heavy reliance on nontax revenue from land resources, and even leniency in enforcing regulations on firms in exchange for tax income. Consequently, new sources of grievance have emerged, further heightening citizens' sensitivity to any tax hikes.

This Element contributes to recent scholarship revisiting the political origins and consequences of fiscal policy and taxation in China.[6] In this strand of

---

[6] Earlier scholarship has either focused on fiscal reforms at the central government level (Shirk 1993; Wang and Hu 1993; Wong and Birds 2008) or fiscal policies at the township and village level (Ong 2012).

literature, they have primarily provided an institutional perspective, highlighting how China's political system and administrative framework shape the development of tax policies and fiscal capacity. For instance, Zhang (2021) contends that the CCP faces two dilemmas concerning taxation – growth and representation – and proposes the pursuit of three sets of strategies to resolve them: Half-tax state,[7] de facto fiscal federalism, and underinstitutionalized tax administration. Focusing on the operation of taxation bureaucracy, Cui (2022) offers a detailed study of the tax administration responsible for tax collection in China. He coins the term "revenue mobilization," arguing that China's expansive tax capacity rests on the revenue management system through non-rule-based tax collection. This observation echoes both qualitative and quantitative studies of fiscal extraction and taxation by subnational governments in China (Lü and Landry 2014; Tian and Zhao 2008; Wu 2007). Lan (2021) places China's fiscal policies in the broader macroeconomic context, studying the ways through which fiscal policies shape local governments' behavior in promoting economic growth, attracting FDI, and expanding urbanization. His argument is built on earlier scholarship indicating that the Chinese government uses fiscal incentives to motivate local governments to pursue industrial growth (Oi 1992). Finally, Lin (2022) provides a comprehensive overview to China's public finance system.

Building on this strand of scholarship, we contend that the evolution of tax reforms since the 1980s reflects a trilemma confronting the central government, which navigated through strategic engagement with local governments. Importantly, we extend the existing institutional perspective by focusing on the *political behaviors* of citizens and businesses in their responses to state tax policies. By leveraging a diverse array of data – from public opinion surveys to instances of social unrest in China – we uncover several new findings. We reveal that urbanites, despite having high tax morale, are highly sensitive to direct taxation and favor redistributive tax policies. In addition, we challenge the presumed link between taxation and social unrest in rural China by highlighting the disparity between trends in social unrest and the peasant tax burden. We suggest that taxation alone may not have been the primary catalyst for rural unrest in the 1990s. Instead, it has been used as leverage by rural residents to vent grievances stemming from issues concerning rural governance. Finally, we observe that businesses in China typically adopt atomized strategies to mitigate their tax burden rather than engaging in collective action to drive broader policy changes. These new insights generate important implications for future studies of taxation and the state–society relationship in China.

---

[7] According to Zhang (2021), the concept of a "half-tax state" highlights China's dependence on nontax revenues, including government fees and contributions from state-owned enterprises. See Section 2.2.1 for a more detailed discussion.

The remainder of this Element is divided into five sections. In Section 2, we offer an overview of China's fiscal system and tax structure, placing it in the global context. Section 3 is a deep dive into the political logic underpinning the evolution of taxation policies in China, emphasizing the distinct objectives and strategies pursued by the central and local governments. We explore both the intention and consequences of several major tax reforms since the 1980s. In Section 4, we shift the focus to the political behaviors of citizens and businesses. Drawing on existing survey data and scholarship, we demonstrate that Chinese citizens exhibit high tax morale and strong expectations for public services in return for taxation. Businesses, by contrast, have sought to secure individual benefits in exchange for taxes. Furthermore, Section 5 highlights several unintended consequences of China's tax policies, focusing on issues like citizens' sensitivity to direct taxation, serious local government debt, heavy reliance on land-based nontax revenue, and the government's leniency in enforcing regulations. In Section 6, we conclude by outlining several promising avenues for further research into the role of taxation in shaping state–society relations in China from a comparative perspective.

2 Lay of the Land: Mapping China's Taxation System and Fiscal Capacity

To contextualize China's contemporary taxation system, we first compare its revenue structure and composition to those of democratic and authoritarian states, then briefly overview its evolution since the reform era. We are primarily interested in a focus on *taxation capacity*, or the state's capacity to collect various forms of taxes, not the broader notion of *fiscal capacity*, or the state's ability to extract revenue from both tax and nontax sources.[8] The distinction reflects state–society relationships through fiscal extraction – from whom and how the state extracts fiscal revenue. For instance, Schumpeter (1991 [1918]) proposed a typology of the state based on the structure of its fiscal revenue: A feudal state is one where rulers fund with their own land, dues paid by their serfs and customs, not by tax. By contrast, a tax state primarily relies on the collection of taxes codified through laws and regulations. Lieberman (2003) expands the categories, identifying five types of fiscal states: Skeletal, rentier, communist, adversarial tax state, and cooperative tax states (54–60). In the

---

[8] A broader definition of fiscal capacity is a state's capacity to use centrally collected (indirect) taxes to mobilize long-term financial resources from the markets (Bonney 1999; He 2013). Emphasizing the importance of borrowing, a marginal definition of fiscal capacity is the ability to issue additional debt in response to a shock (Botev, Fournier, and Mourougane, 2016). We do not discuss fiscal capacity in this way in this Element.

rentier state and the communist state, a state may have high fiscal capacity but low taxation capacity.

The hallmark of a modern fiscal state is reliance on taxation as its primary source of revenue, offering legitimacy and transparency to the state's fiscal extraction. Since the reform era of the 1980s, the Chinese government has pursued rapid economic growth while strengthening its fiscal capacity. Alongside this process, China's fiscal regime evolved from a communist state to a tax state, mirroring its broader transition from a planned economy to a socialist market economy. In particular, the Chinese government has undertaken a series of fiscal reforms to strengthen its taxation institutions since the early 1990s, aligning with a broader transition to a market economy.[9] Slowly, China's tax-to-GDP ratio steadily rebounded from less than 10% in 1994 to over 20% by 2020. We conclude by examining a key characteristic of its tax state – reliance on indirect taxation – and place it in the larger context of nontax revenues and contributions from state-owned enterprises (SOEs).

2.1 Tax Capacities and Structures of Autocracies and Democracies

According to Huntington (1968) the *effectiveness* of government is a more critical concern for developing countries than its *form*, but the reverse also holds true: The forms of government can significantly influence the capacity and effectiveness of governance, particularly in tax capacity. To this end, researchers attempt to identify the causal effect of regime type on taxation capacity, yet empirical findings remain inclusive.

From one perspective, democracies may tax less than autocracies because institutional arrangements like elections and legislatures generate veto points constraining ruling governments' ability to extract revenue from society at will (Tsebelis 2002). Furthermore, democratic governments generally rely less on coercion, leading to lower tax rates than authoritarian governments with the means and incentives to impose onerous tax burdens on citizens (Przeworski 1990).

Another perspective suggests the opposite: Democracies are associated with higher taxation.[10] Facing the pressure of median voters, democracies may tax more for redistribution, especially in countries rife with inequality (Meltzer and Richard 1981). Democracies could also tax more because of heavier investment in building taxation capacity (Besley, Ilzetzki, and Persson 2013). Finally, an effective taxation system relies on quasivoluntary tax compliance, or compliance

---

[9] See Section 3 for a series of important tax reforms by the Chinese government for this endeavor.
[10] See Andersen and Ross (2014), Prichard, Salardi, and Segal (2014), Ross (2004), and Wiens, Poast, and Clark (2014).

motivated by a willingness to cooperate but backed by coercion (Levi 2006: 7). Because of representative institutions and government transparency, democracies have a stronger capacity to achieve citizens' quasivoluntary compliance, embodying higher taxation capacity than authoritarian regimes.

Empirical investigations, however, demonstrate a mixed relationship between regime type and taxation capacity. Whereas Garcia and von Haldenwang (2016) identify a nonlinear relationship between tax ratios and democracy scores, Cheibub (1998), Herb (2005), and Mulligan, Gil, and Sala-i Martin (2004) find no difference in the taxation capacity of democracies and autocracies. Using longer time-series data, Haber and Menaldo (2011) find no significant relationship between tax reliance and regime type.

The mixed evidence on the relationship between regime type and fiscal capacity may derive from several critical factors shaping taxation capacity. Besley and Persson (2011) suggest investment in fiscal capacity as a forward-looking decision by ruling elites, influenced by the costs of investment and uncertainty surrounding future benefits. Key determinants of these cost–benefit analyses include the state of the regime (i.e., common-interest states, redistributive states, and weak states), degree of political stability, resource (aid) independence, and level of economic development. Rather than adhering to a simplistic dichotomy of regime types, their framework underscores the interplay of political, economic, and cultural factors shaping a country's fiscal capacity. Importantly, they emphasize the complementariness in development clusters of these factors. Shown later, this approach offers valuable insights into China's fiscal capacity development, yet puzzling patterns remain.

Turning to case studies, Bräutigam, Fjeldstad, and Moore (2008) and Moore, Prichard, and Fjeldstad (2018) highlight a complex web of tax capacity determinants. Building on recent elite-centric accounts of taxation capacity, the former underscore the development of a state's taxation capacity, primarily shaped by the incentives and capabilities of ruling elites in state-capacity building.[11] Furthermore, a state's commitment to economic development and distinctive economic model also yields significant implications for the evolution of its taxation capacity. Demonstrated in Section 2.2.1, China's SOEs and land-based revenue play a unique role in strengthening the government's taxation capacity within a competitive market system – an exceptional case among autocracies that typically rely on indirect taxation and natural resource revenues to sustain fiscal capacity (Morrison 2015; Ross 2012).

Finally, Stasavage (2016) contends that the rise of representation and expansion of fiscal capacity in premodern Europe is conditional on a unique historical

---

[11] See, for example, Besley and Persson (2009), Brewer (1989), and Dincecco (2011).

context. On one hand, representation improves the quality of public expenditure, thus contributing to economic growth. On the other hand, representative institutions improve taxation capacity by improving tax compliance without producing political instability. Most developing countries today, however, encounter limited interstate warfare and easy access to nontax revenue sources. Consequently, rulers have weaker incentives to invest in costly taxation capacity (Centeno 2002; Herbst 2000; Moore 2008; Queralt 2022). Considering the potential political demand stemming from expanding taxation capacity, Martin (2023) argues that rent-seeking leaders in low-capacity states strategically underinvest in fiscal capacity to reduce citizens' call for political representation and accountability. Similarly, Slater, Smith, and Nair (2014) note that many newly established democracies struggle with building the infrastructural capacity needed for effective resource extraction, particularly in taxing the wealthy, largely because these governments tend to limit political contestation.

2.1.1 China's Taxation Capacity in a Comparative Perspective

With the caveat that the relationship between regime type and taxation is mixed in existing studies, we compare China's taxation in the global context. First, we place a commonly used measure of taxation capacity – ratio of tax revenue to GDP – against the level of economic development of the country. Taxation data derive from the International Centre for Tax and Development (ICTD);[12] the measure of GDP, from Fariss et al. (2022). We drew the measure of regime type from the political regime indicator on the *Varieties of Democracy* (V-dem).[13]

We first plot the ratio of tax revenue to GDP against GDP per capita (PPP, purchasing power parity) for all countries in 2018, marking them by regime type and adding a linear fitted value for each type. Figure 1 reveals three patterns. First, the ratio of tax revenue to GDP positively correlates with GDP per capita income as predicted by Wagner's law (Besley and Persson 2011; Easterly and Rebelo 1993). Second, democratic regimes tend to have higher taxation capacity compared to autocracies as the level of economic development increases. Democratic regimes average 21.26% in terms of the ratio of tax revenue to GDP, with a median of 21.03%; authoritarian regimes average 15.21%, with a median of 14.55%. China's taxation capacity aligns with a typical authoritarian regime at 18.52%, sitting above the fitted value for authoritarian regimes but below the fitted value for democracies. Third, we observe significant variations within and

---

[12] We use the variable "tax_ex_sc," or taxes excluding social contribution, from the ICTD dataset in 2018 (www.ictd.ac/).

[13] We use the variable "v2x_polyarchy" from V-dem website (https://v-dem.net/) in 2018 and code the political regime as a democratic regime if the v2x_polyarchy is equal to or greater than 0.5. Otherwise, the political regime is coded as an authoritarian regime.

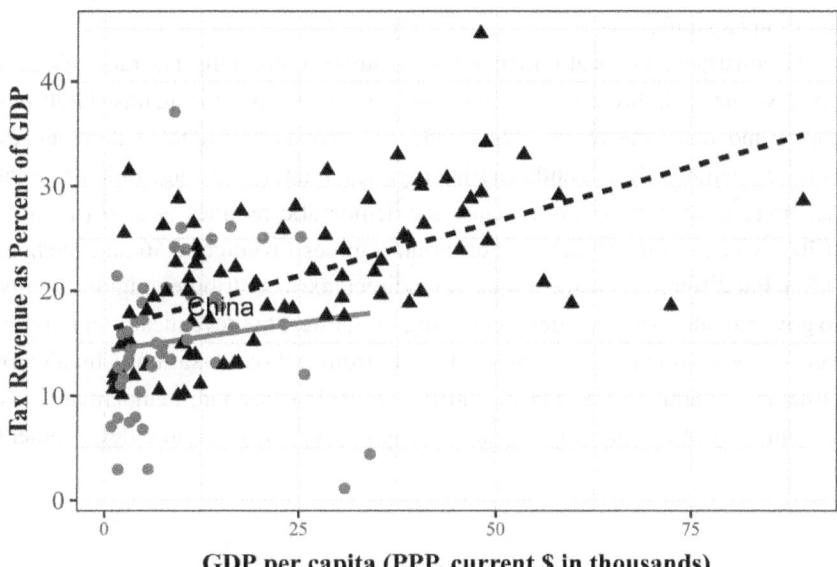

Figure 1 Ratio of tax revenue to GDP among autocracies and democracies (2018).

Note: The tax revenue data are from ICDT. The data of GDP per capita are from Fariss, Anders, Markowitz & Barnum (2022). Finally, we rely on V-dem for the definition of regime type.

across regime types, consistent with mixed findings in existing studies and the framework built by Besley and Persson (2011), emphasizing the complementarities of development clusters.

2.1.2 China's Taxation Structure in a Comparative Perspective

The structure of direct and indirect taxation is another revealing indicator for the state of taxation capacity. Direct taxation refers to taxes imposed on individuals and firms based on their income and assets, including personal and business income taxes, property taxes, and inheritance tax. Indirect taxation is levied on goods and services, including VAT, sales taxes, and customs on imports and exports. Of the two, direct taxation poses a greater challenge for any state because it demands a robust bureaucratic capacity for accurate assessment and effective compliance (Rothstein 2011; Prasad 2018); moreover, it is far more salient than indirect taxation because of its visibility, thus engendering greater political resistance (Finkelstein 2009; Martin 2023;

Prasad 2012). Given the challenges and complexity of the collection, direct taxation has been commonly considered a benchmark for measuring a state's taxation capacity.

We construct an indicator to measure a state's tax structure: The ratio of direct tax revenue to indirect tax revenue. We plot this indicator against GDP per capita and mark the regime type. Figure 2 reveals two notable divergences between democratic and authoritarian regimes. First, the average ratio of direct tax revenue to indirect tax revenue for democratic regimes is 0.90 (median, 0.70), which is higher than authoritarian regimes (average, 0.56 and median, 0.52). Put differently, while direct and indirect taxes contribute roughly equally to government revenue in democratic regimes, direct tax revenues in authoritarian regimes amount to only 56% of those from indirect taxation. China's tax structure remains in the mix of autocracies (0.58). Second, democracies' tax structures increasingly rely on direct taxation as their economic development

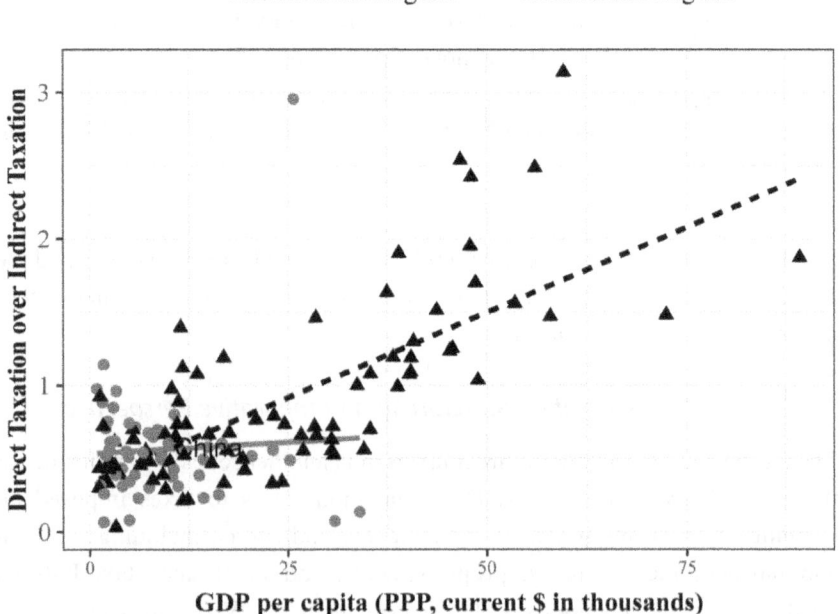

Figure 2 The ratio of direct to indirect taxation among autocracies and democracies (2018)

Note: The tax revenue data are from ICDT. The data of GDP per capita are from Fariss, Anders, Markowitz & Barnum (2022). Finally, we rely on V-dem for the definition of regime type.

advances.[14] By contrast, little correlation exists between tax structure and the level of economic development in autocracies.

Figures 1 and 2 suggest that democracies and autocracies may pursue different strategies for building taxation capacity. Specifically, the taxation capacity of democratic regimes is positively associated with reliance on direct taxation. By contrast, autocratic regimes demonstrate no clear preference for either direct or indirect taxation; if anything, they may deliberately limit the expansion of direct taxation to minimize potential conflicts in state–society relations.

2.2 The Evolution of China's Fiscal Capacity since the Reform Era

Section 2.1 reveals that China's taxation capacity aligns with global norms given its level of economic development, marked by a significant reliance on indirect taxation. But how has China's tax system evolved since the 1980s? Furthermore, what is the relative contribution of tax vis-à-vis nontax revenue to China's fiscal capacity? In Section 2.2, we review the evolution of tax capacity and structure within the broader context of China's fiscal capacity.

2.2.1 Structure and Sources of Fiscal Revenue

We first examine the shifting primary sources of fiscal revenue since the 1980s. Zhang (2021) calls China's fiscal state a "half-tax state," relying on indirect taxes (comprising two-thirds of tax revenue) and nontax revenue as the primary sources of government income. Furthermore, SOEs still play a vital role in contributing to both tax and nontax revenue despite China's transition from a planned to market economy.

The complexity of fiscal revenue definitions employed by the Chinese government reflects its evolving fiscal capacity since the reform era (Table 1). For instance, *General Public Budget Revenue* encompasses most funds allocated for public expenditure. Notably, the Chinese central government has sought to curtail local governments' extrabudgetary incomes (预算外收入) since the 2000s by integrating them into *General Public Budget Revenue* to enhance oversight. In addition, the central government designated the *Government Fund* to provide regulation and oversee government-led infrastructure investment and social development initiatives. The reform of China's social security system established the *Social Security Fund*. Last, the government designated an account – *State Capital Operations Income* – to manage revenue from SOE remittance.

---

[14] Note that Beramendi and Rueda (2007) find that social democratic states improve taxation capacity mostly based on indirect taxes.

Table 1 Definition and source of fiscal revenue

Fiscal revenue	Definition	Sources of revenue
General Public Budget Revenue (一般预算收入)	Revenue and expenditure budget to ensure people's livelihood, promote economic and social development, safeguard national security, and maintain normal operation of state institutions	Tax revenue; nontax revenue (e.g., administrative fees; income from confiscation, franchises, the Central Bank, donations received in the name of the government, government departments, interest on government revenue); debts and fiscal transfers (for local governments only)
Government Fund (政府基金)	Income obtained by the state for specific purposes: infrastructure building and social development	Income from compensated use of state-owned resources (assets) (i.e., land transfer fees), revenue from project-specific bonds and lottery public welfare funds
State Capital Operations Income (国有资本经营)	Revenue from government acquisition of state-owned capital gains by law as the owner and distribution of gains	Profit remittance and transfers from state-owned capital, transfer of state capital, liquidation income from SOEs
Social Security Fund (社保基金)	Social security contributions exclusively for social insurance	Social security income and fiscal transfer

Source: Ma and Zhao (2019): 205–210.

Based on these definitions, we illustrate the changes in China's fiscal capacity from 1990 to 2023 in Figure 3. First, the share of tax revenue as a percent of GDP rose from less than 10% in 1995 to as high as 17% around 2013, retreating to 15% in 2023. Turning to *General Public Budget Revenue*, including some nontax revenues, we find a slightly higher level of fiscal capacity. Its share of GDP hovered around 10% in 1995, surged to over 22% by 2015, retreating to just over 17% in 2023. If we adopt a broader definition of government revenue (*Total Revenue*), which includes all four types of revenue noted in Table 1, it reached as high as 35%, declining to only 30% in recent years.

Taxation and Governance in Contemporary China 13

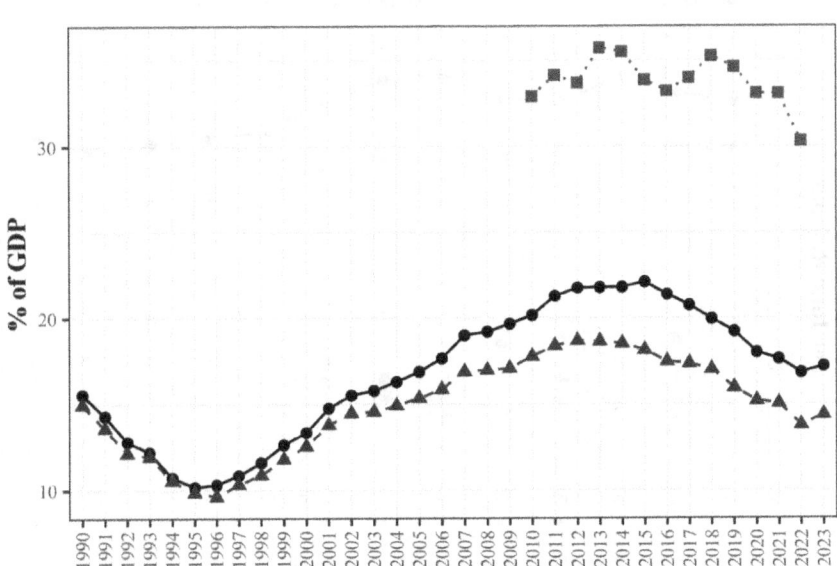

Figure 3 Fiscal capacity through various definitions (1990–2023).
Note: Data derived from the *China Statistical Yearbook*.

To further unpack the contribution from nontax revenues, Figure 4 illustrates the share of government revenue from various sources. Specifically, the share of *General Public Budget Revenue* has amounted to over 60% of the total government revenue since 2010, beginning a decline to 53% in 2021. Meanwhile, the share of the *Government Fund* and the *Social Security Fund* rose to 26% and 20% of total government revenue in 2021, respectively. If land transfer fees are separated from the *Government Fund*, Figure 4 shows that they became a significant source of revenue for Chinese local governments from early 2000s to 2020, and only recent economic woes resulted in the sharp decline that contributed to the growing revenue challenges faced by local governments. Together, these measures of fiscal capacity indicate that although tax revenue constitutes the major fiscal income source for the Chinese government, nontax revenues – government funds, social security, and state capital operations income – have increased since 2015.

Now we turn to a narrower definition of fiscal revenue – tax revenue. As in many nondemocratic regimes, China's taxation capacity predominantly relies on indirect taxation, constituting approximately two-thirds of total tax revenue. In Figure 5, we deconstruct tax revenue by sources and trace their

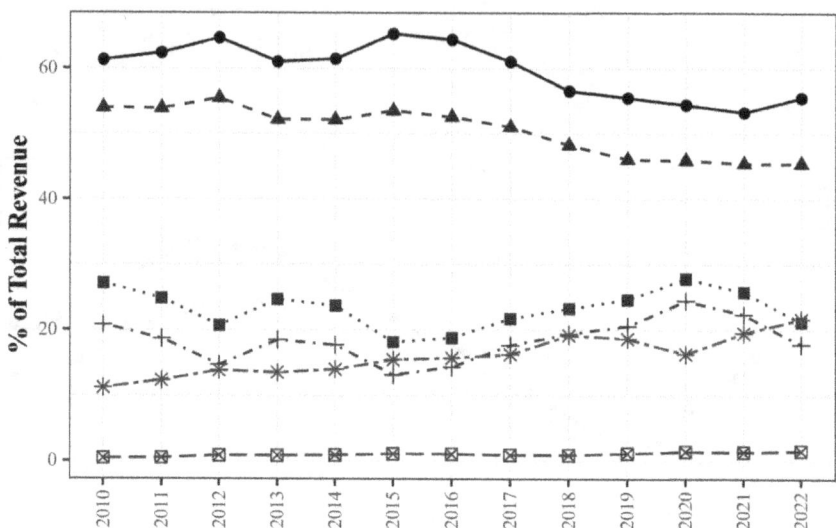

Figure 4 Share of revenue from various sources (2010–2022).

Note: Data derived from the *China Statistical Yearbook*. Tax revenue is a major subcategory of *General Public Budget Revenue*; land transfer fees constitute a major subcategory of the *Government Fund*. The Social Security Fund excludes the fiscal transfer fund (from General Public Budget Revenue).

contribution to overall tax revenue from 1990 to 2023. The VAT emerges as the most important –its share in the total tax revenue consistently above 30% after the 1994 TSS reform. Although that figure has gradually declined since the late 2000s because of the rising contribution from personal and corporate income tax, it returned to become the primary source of tax revenue, especially after the BT (business tax)-to-VAT reform in 2016.[15] Meanwhile, corporate income tax has consistently risen since 2000, reaching 25% of total tax revenue by 2023. Personal income tax and domestic consumption have remained minimal, each contributing less than 10% of government revenue over time.

2.2.2 Fiscal Contribution from SOEs

A large, strong sector of SOEs makes a unique contribution to Chinese fiscal capacity. First, despite decades of market reform, SOEs and state-holding

---

[15] The sharp increase in the VAT share in 2023 occurred because of the VAT credit refund and tax deduction policy in 2022 that reduced the baseline for overall tax revenue that year.

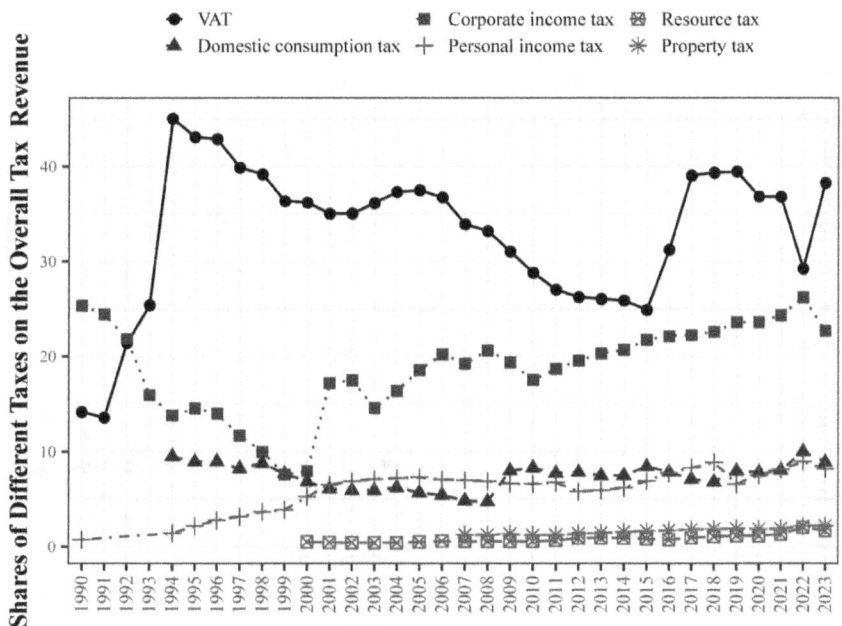

Figure 5 China's structure of tax revenue (1990–2023).

Note: Data derived from the *China Statistical Yearbook*. The drop in VAT in 2021 occurred because the VAT allowance for refund policy was designed to stimulate economic growth during the COVID pandemic.

corporations are a major source of national tax revenue, contributing 31.7% of government revenue in 2014 whereas collective enterprises and collective holdings, about 34% (Zhang 2021: 56). Notably, the substantial tax contribution by SOEs can be attributed to their monopoly in sectors like energy, utilities, and finance.

Second, SOE profit remittance, comprising half the national fiscal revenue before 1980, has been replaced by taxes as a consequence of 1984 and 1985 tax-for-profit reforms (Figures 6a and 6b). The SOE profit remittance drastically declined from 1993 to 2006 because of the dismal performance of most SOEs in the 1990s and early 2000s.

Nonetheless, SOEs reemerged as a major force in the Chinese economy, an increasingly important fiscal revenue source.[16] From 2013 to 2022, a total of 18.2 trillion yuan was submitted by central SOEs (央企) through taxes and fees, accounting for about one-eighth of the national tax revenue: 1.3 trillion yuan to state capital operation income and another 1.2 trillion yuan to the *Social*

---

[16] For the rise and fall of SOEs in the Chinese economy, see, for example, Huang (2008) and Lardy (2014, 2019). Pearson, Rithmire, and Tsai (2023) offer an excellent review.

(a) Sources of fiscal revenue

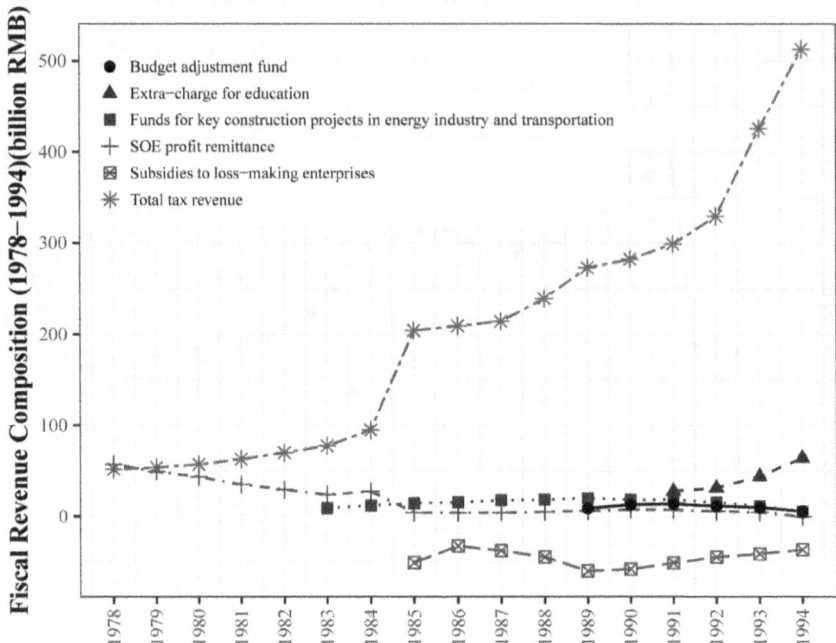

(b) Tax revenue and share of fiscal revenue from SOE remittance

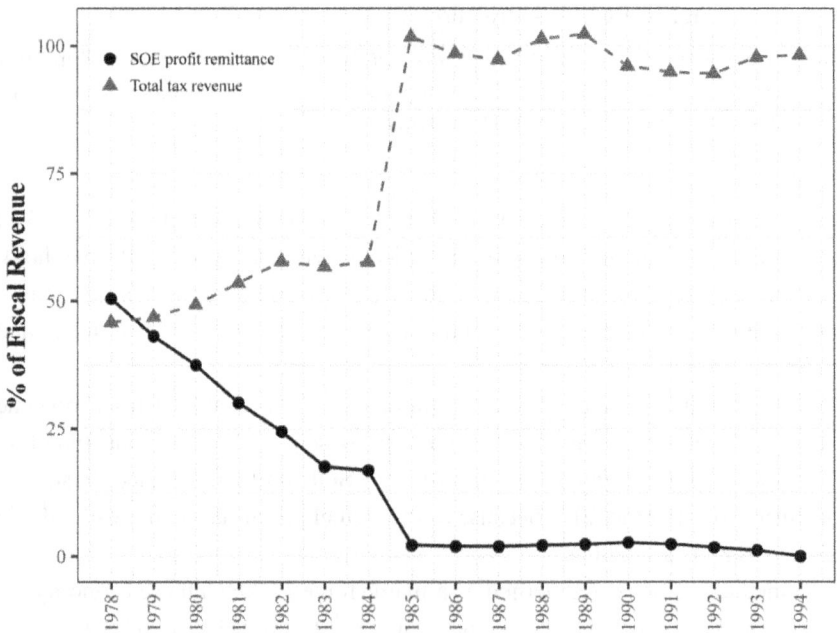

Figure 6 SOEs fiscal contribution (1978–1994)

Notes: Data derived from *China Statistical Yearbook*. The SOE profit remittance was suspended in 1994, so the sum of shares in (b) does not equal or exceed 100 because of other revenue sources and subsidies to lose-making SOEs (negative). Fiscal revenue here refers to General Public Budgetary Revenue.

Security Fund.[17] Notably, only the profits of nonfinancial SOEs are included in the state capital operations budget as profit submission and are then used to supplement General Public Budget Revenue through the transfer of funds. The profits submitted by financial SOEs are not included in state capital operations income but are managed by the Ministry of Finance (MOF) separately and included in the nontax revenue of *General Public Budget Revenue*. However, central SOEs' profit remittance is still very limited compared to their profits. For example, central SOEs had a total profit of 2.55 trillion yuan and submitted 2.8 trillion as taxes and fees in 2022, while SOEs' profit remittance contributed only 172 billion yuan to state capital operation income.[18] This contribution should be discounted as the government returns most profits submitted by SOEs through reinvestment, therefore contributing even less to fiscal revenue.

In addition to the two routine channels, the Chinese central government mandates specific state-owned financial and franchised institutions, such as the China National Tobacco Corporation, to remit their accumulated profits in a lump sum (as nontax revenue) during periods of economic hardship. The profits should be transferred to the government-managed fund budget as 'special profits turned over by central government units' and transferred to the general public budget as needed. In 2022, for example, the People's Bank of China, its central bank, turned over 1.13 trillion yuan in surplus profits to the country's central budget to "support enterprises, stabilize employment and ensure people's well-being."[19]

2.3 Administrative Foundation of China's Taxation Capacity

Developing a strong bureaucratic capacity for taxation is a challenging task for any country, and China is no exception. Since its transition to a market economy in the 1980s, the Chinese government launched several waves of reform to strengthen its taxation capacity. In this section, we briefly overview the evolution of China's tax administration since the 1980s,[20] then discuss a unique practice of China's tax administration – the tax targeting system – which allows the Chinese Central Government to ensure compliance from low-level government in tax collection.

---

[17] State-Owned Assets Supervision and Administration Commission, 2023. "Report of Central SOEs' High-Quality Development 2022." www.sasac.gov.cn/n2588020/n2877938/n2879671/n2879673/c26508617/content.html.

[18] www.sasac.gov.cn/n4470048/n26915116/n28915164/n28915194/c28940209/content.html.

[19] "Xinhua, China's central bank to provide 1t yuan to central budget" (March 9, 2022). https://english.www.gov.cn/statecouncil/ministries/202203/09/content_WS6227e373c6d09c94e48a64ad.html (accessed September 13, 2024).

[20] Cui (2022) offers an excellent study of China's tax administration.

2.3.1 Evolution of the Tax Administration

China decentralized its tax administration in the 1980s to operate as a subsidiary of the MOF. Thus, local tax bureaus were directly managed by corresponding local finance bureaus and, by extension, local party and government authorities – a structure known as horizontal management.[21] The state administration of taxation was a semi-ministerial-level agency at the national level under the MOF but lacking direct power to command tax bureaus at the provincial level, which were controlled by provincial governments. Under this arrangement, tax administration was decentralized to local governments, which collected tax revenue and then remitted part of it to higher-level governments.

The 1994 Tax Sharing System (TSS) reform was designed to institutionalize spending obligations and tax sharing between central and local governments, specifically to recentralize the taxation power. To facilitate tax collection, the TSS reform established two independent and vertically managed taxation bureaus: The State Administration of Taxation (SAT) and the Local Taxation Bureau (LTB). The SAT falls under the direct leadership of the Chinese Central Government (State Council) as a ministerial-level institution. Although the SAT is independent from the MOF, the personnel of these two agencies maintain close working relationships. For instance, SAT directors usually have prior experience at the MOF before their appointments. Although the SAT was institutionally independent from the local government, LTBs operated under dual leadership, reporting to both the higher-level LTBs and local governments in jurisdictions where they are located. Notably, the higher-level LTBs – or the SAT in the case of a provincial-level LTB – had greater administrative authority in appointing local LTB directors and supervising their size and organizational issues.

Both the size and capacity of China's tax administration experienced rapid growth after the 1994 TSS reform. Together, the SAT and LTB employ about one million people; furthermore, both are equipped with more professionals than their predecessors, up-to-date information technology and equipment, a rationalized management system, and an improved taxation capacity. In 2018, the SAT and LTB were merged into the new SAT, designed to further streamline tax collection and improve administrative efficiency. In addition, the *Social Security Fund* collection was assigned to the new SAT. Compared to the Bureau of Human Resources and the Social Security Administration, the new SAT now has a much greater capacity for fee collection, further strengthening

---

[21] See Yang (2004) on China's administrative reform and the difference between vertical and horizontal management systems.

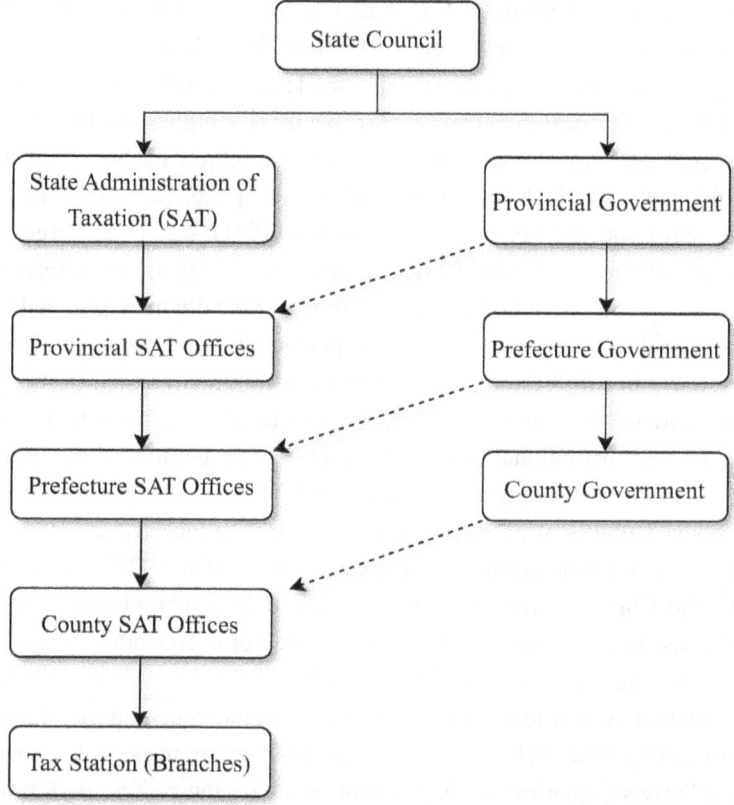

Figure 7 Organizational structures of tax administrations in China (2018–Present).

Notes: This figure is based on Figure 5 in Cui (2022: 170), but we provide a more detailed demonstration of the relationships among levels of government and SATs at several levels.

its taxation capacity. Figure 7 reflects the organizational structure of China's tax administration after 2018.

2.3.2 The Tax Target System

Despite the Chinese government's endeavor to transition into a modern tax state through these major fiscal reforms, its taxation system retains an important legacy of the previous fiscal system under the planned economy and the unitary system – the tax target system – for the purpose of revenue mobilization (Cui 2022). Although the Chinese government has maintained the importance of

Rule by Law,[22] many tax liabilities are not in fact designated by law (依法征税) but according to the revenue targets set by their supervisors (higher-level tax bureaus and governments at the corresponding levels) and informal agreements between tax administrators and taxpayers. Specifically, higher-level tax bureaus and the local governments set specific tax revenue targets for both the county SAT office, within which all the tax collection agents (tax office and tax officials) have specific tax collection targets (税收任务). These targets are reminiscent of the fiscal contracting system that the 1994 TSS reform was intended to replace. Notably, the tax bureaus are vertically managed, and local governments do not have the power of personnel management to directly pressure SATs to fulfill these targets. Instead, a common method to motivate local tax bureaus is financial reward;[23] consequently, the tax target system undermines the institutionalization of tax collection because it violates the rule of law in the realm of taxation (Zhang 2021).

The primary objective of the tax target system is to incentivize tax bureaucrats at various levels to enhance tax collection efforts (Cui 2022; Zhang 2021). Notably, the Chinese government has a decentralized administrative system given its vast territory, and local politicians are not accountable to residents because of the lack of meaningful elections. The CCP developed a nomenklatura system to use career incentives to motivate and monitor local officials (Landry 2008; Whiting 2004). Local CCP committees, with assistance from the Party's Organization Department, evaluate the cadres' performance and punish or reward them through a cadre management system[24] that covers economic growth, tax revenue, social stability, environmental protection, and population control. These metrics are adjusted from periodically, depending on the Party's political priorities. Organizations and individuals accomplishing or exceeding the target are rewarded both economically (bonus) and politically (better opportunity for promotion).[25] Notably, local cadres view nomenklatura as a pressure-based system (压力型体制) (Rong 1998). In the realm of taxation, revenue targets are divided into smaller quotas and assigned to lower-level government organizations or individuals expected to meet these targets within a specified timeframe.[26]

---

[22] The People's Republic of China implemented the Law on the Administration of Tax Collection on January 1, 1993. For more discussion of rule-by-law taxation, see Cui (2022).
[23] See Zhang (2021: 86–90) and Cui (2022: 164–173).
[24] See Edin (2003) and Landry (2008) for the cadre management system.
[25] For taxation targets as career incentives, see Lü and Landry (2014) and Landry, Lü, and Duan (2018).
[26] Cui (2022: 153) provides details of measuring tax bureaus' performances.

2.4 Conclusion

This section maps out China's taxation system within the broader context of fiscal capacity. To some extent, China's rising fiscal capacity since the reform era aligns with the predictions in the theoretical framework proposed by Besley and Persson's (2011). Unlike the Maoist period (1949–1976), the reform era has been characterized by prolonged political stability, rising per capita income, and cohesive political institutions committed to a common objective – economic development. China's taxation capacity development, however, diverges from this framework in notable ways, particularly in the government's reluctance to expand direct taxation. Instead, it has persistently relied on indirect taxation and nontax revenues as the primary source of fiscal revenue. In the next section, we explore the political logic behind the design of China's tax system and tax reforms, demonstrating how strategic interactions between the central and local governments have been pivotal in its evolution. In Sections 4 and 5, we examine how China's taxation system influences the behaviors of local governments, citizens, and businesses as well as the dynamics of their interactions.

3 Political Logic of Taxation in China

> *Our country is so large with such an enormous population, and the situation is so complicated, with both central and local initiatives, which are much better than having only one initiative.... We should promote the style of handling affairs in consultation with the local authorities. When handling affairs, the Center should always consult with the local authorities and never give orders blindly without consulting with different authorities.*
>
> Mao Zedong, 1956, "On Ten Major Relationships"

Taxation manifests the state's endeavor to extract economic resources from the society, making it a focal point for state–society tensions. Arising from fiscal policies, conflicts in democracies are often mediated through electoral competition, where tax policy design reflects the aggregation of mass preferences shaped not only by voters' self-interest but also by the influence of political and economic elites on public opinion. By contrast, policymaking in autocracies is typically insulated from public scrutiny and interparty competition, rendering a different logic behind the design of tax policy.

Although the CCP remains the dominant ruling party with supreme authority in the political system, it gradually delegated the design and implementation of economic policies to the government apparatus, reflecting a fundamental shift in its priorities from political struggle to economic development.[27] Shirk (1993) underscores the institutional contours (i.e., the separation of the party and state in economic policymaking and the political competition among elites striving for political appointment) as key drivers behind China's economic and fiscal reforms. Importantly, Shirk proposes a selectorate model,[28] in which "reciprocal accountability" exists among elites holding leadership positions in the party, government, and military. Although high-level officials are appointed by the CCP Politburo and its Standing Committee, they wield significant influence in shaping the competition among party leaders vying for ascension to the very pinnacle of China's political hierarchy. Policymaking in China, therefore, is essentially a process of elite bargaining and factional struggle, engineered by high-level elite CCP members who seek support from leaders in ministerial bureaucracies and provincial governments.

This logic is reflected by the characterization of China's policymaking process from the perspective of "fragmented authoritarianism" (Lieberthal 1992; Lieberthal and Oksenberg 1988), revealing that the Chinese government is not a monolith but a complex system comprising multiple political elites, each overseeing distinct policy domains. These political leaders have conflictual or complementary policy goals, and policy outcomes reflect the distribution of power and coalition building among them. The authority structure became decentralized and fragmented after Mao; therefore, policymaking now requires building a unified consensus within bureaucratic systems. Consequently, the policymaking process results from governmental bargaining and consensus building by *horizontal* bureaucracies (ministries) with "department parochialism" and *vertical* government agencies (local party government) with "local protectionism."

Among the layers of governmental relations, central–local interaction plays a vital role in shaping China's tax policies. Effective fiscal centralization is considered a hallmark of the modern tax state (Dincecco 2009), but it is not only about placing the power of tax policymaking into the hands of the central government, which may hold de jure authority in designing and legislating tax policies. Local governments, however, maintain de facto power in policy implementation; therefore, the central government must be mindful of their

---

[27] See Vogel (2011) for a study of Deng Xiaoping, widely considered the architect of China's economic reform. For the origins of China's economic reform, see Lieberthal (2004) and Shirk (1993).

[28] Defined as the body with the power to select and remove policy makers, the selectorate model was developed to facilitate discussion of the relationship between the leader and the party bureaucracy in post-Stalin communism.

preferences and negotiate with them during the policymaking process to ensure smooth policy implementation.

Viewing tax policies through the lens of central–local relations, we investigate the central and local governments' fiscal policy goals and behaviors, particularly in the realm of taxation. We show that the central government faces a trilemma of revenue extraction, economic growth, and political stability, employing legislative power and career advancement to incentivize local governments to achieve their objectives. Meanwhile, local governments, broadly aligned with central government objectives like economic development and revenue generation, selectively implement tax policies to advance their own interests. Given the short time horizon of local governments, their policy choices often engender political instability or deviations from the objectives of the central government, worsening the trilemma faced by the latter. In the context of the trilemma, we then briefly discuss the motivation and outcomes of several major fiscal and tax reforms in China since the 1980s.

3.1 Central Government Trilemma: Balancing Multiple Policy Goals

What does the Chinese central government seek to accomplish through its tax policies? Bolstering the state's fiscal capacity through tax revenue is the most obvious objective. In addition, the Chinese government considers tax revenue an important instrument for stimulating economic growth, particularly through government capital investment and public goods provision. Finally, maintaining political stability is the foremost concern for any single-party regime. Hence, the Chinese government must carefully considers the direct and indirect impact of its tax policies on political stability. These policy goals were explicitly laid out in the Communiqué of the Third Plenary Session of the 18th Central Committee of the CCP in 2018: [Public] finance is the foundation and an important pillar of state governance. Good fiscal and taxation systems are the institutional guarantee for optimizing resources allocation, maintaining market unity, promoting social equity, and realizing enduring peace and stability.[29]

Some governments invest in expanding taxation capacity and strengthening representative institutions, leading to the formation of a "developmental cluster," where high taxation, political stability, and a high level of development could coexist (Besley and Persson 2011). Representative institutions aggregate mass preferences and translate them into public expenditure, which in turn promotes economic growth, enhances tax compliance, and strengthens regime legitimacy.

---

[29] See www.china.org.cn/chinese/2014-01/16/content_31213800_2.htm (accessed on August 15, 2024).

Meanwhile, nondemocratic regimes could achieve revenue extraction, economic growth, and expanded public spending to maintain political stability (Acemoglu 2005; Morrison 2015). These outcomes are, however, often sustained through nontax revenues like natural resource endowments. In the absence of representative institutions and abundant natural resources in China, balancing these three policy goals poses an acute challenge. Scholars have documented local governments prioritizing economic growth at the expense of environmental protection and labor relations.[30] When the Chinese government expands social welfare to ease state–society tensions stemming from rapid economic growth and rising inequality, its policies have yielded limited improvements in citizen trust (Li et al. 2025; Lü 2014; Yang and Shen 2021), sometimes even serving as instruments of surveillance and repression (Pan 2020).

Equally important, Besley and Persson (2011) underscore the cohesiveness of political institutions as pivotal in shaping fiscal capacity, alongside other complementary elements in the development clusters. The institutional design of China's central–local relations creates conflicting interests between central and local leaders. For instance, the 1994 TSS reform enabled the central government to retain most of the revenue surplus, leaving local governments grappling with persistent budgetary constraints. This is exacerbated by pervasive unfunded mandates, compelling local authorities to implement policies without necessary financial support, further straining their fiscal resources (Wong and Bird 2008). Meanwhile, economic growth has been a cornerstone of the CCP's "performance legitimacy," crucial in maintaining popular support (Dickson 2016; Zhao 2009). The emphasis on promoting economic development, however, prevents the government from imposing heavy tax burdens onto firms, which sometimes even receive illicit tax breaks from local governments. Similarly, efforts to expand public goods and social welfare may support political stability in the short term, but they could strain fiscal resources and hinder long-term economic growth if improperly managed.

Figure 8 illustrates the trilemma the Chinese government faces concerning the delicate balance among these policy goals. In the remainder of this section, we first highlight the importance of these three policy goals to the Chinese central government. We then discuss the ways the central government addresses the tradeoffs among them through tax systems and policy adjustments. In Section 3.3, we offer a nuanced discussion on how specific reforms prioritized one aspect of the trilemma while generating unintended consequences for the others.

---

[30] See Section 5 for more details.

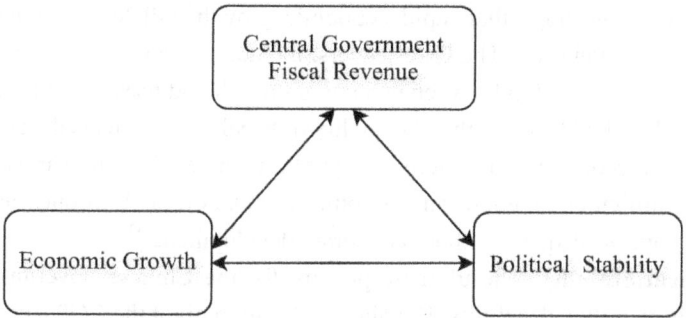

Figure 8 The trilemma among policy goals

3.1.1 Central Government's Objectives

Fiscal Revenue. "Revenue enhances the ability of rulers to elaborate the institutions of the state, to bring more people within the domain of those institutions, and to increase the number and variety of the collective goods provided through the state" (Levi 1988: 2). Fiscal revenue is indispensable for any state – including the CCP – in performing government functions. As a late industrializing country, the CCP pursued the model of a planned economy in the 1950s by following that of the Soviet Union and taxed the peasants heavily to support rapid industrialization. After the 1994 TSS reform, increased tax revenue empowered the central government to finance important initiatives – capital investment, national defense, and intergovernmental transfers as well as the expansion of the provision of public goods and services in the last two decades. During economic downturns, the central government often becomes the ultimate, if not the sole, source of emergency spending to stimulate the economy and provide bailouts for financially struggling local governments. Notably, the central government aims to maintain macroeconomic stability while promoting economic growth. Before the transition to a market economy, the Chinese government relied on administrative tools but not fiscal and financial policies for macroeconomic management (Huang 1996). After transitioning to a market economy, fiscal policies became a more effective tool for macroeconomic management (Liu and Fu 2018: 165).

Economic Growth. Recognizing the importance of performance legitimacy as a substitute for charismatic legitimacy, the CCP shifted its focus from class struggle to economic development in the late 1970s. Deng Xiaoping (1983: 214) famously said, "Development is the absolute principle," acknowledging that bringing prosperity to the people would revive popular support for the CCP after years of political and economic turmoil from 1949 to 1978. The Chinese government prioritizes promoting economic growth by maintaining a light tax burden, with the hope that rapid economic growth will lead to greater tax revenue in the long run. The CCP leaders, including Mao Zedong, recognized the intricate relationship between economic growth and fiscal revenue as early as 1942. He said: "It is true that the quality of fiscal policy affects the economy, but it is the economy that determines public finances. No one can solve the financial difficulties without an economic foundation, and no one can make public finances adequate without economic development."[31]

Political Stability. The ultimate priority for the Chinese government has always been political stability. Despite his desire to pivot the CCP's priority to promoting economic growth, Deng Xiaoping reminded party leaders that "[political] stability is a principle of overriding importance" (Deng 1993: 363). Facing mounting social discontents stemming from two decades of economic reforms, the Hu Jintao and Wen Jiabao administration shifted the national development priority in the mid-2000s from solely promoting economic growth to implementing the so-called "scientific outlook of development" (科学发展观) along with a "harmonious society (和谐社会)," emphasizing more expenditures on public goods provision. Meanwhile, stability maintenance became an increasingly pressing issue for the CCP, eventually leading to the establishment of a costly stability maintenance system under the leadership of Zhou Yongkang, then a standing committee member of the Politburo in charge of the Central Politics and Law Commission. Despite Zhou's downfall during Xi Jinping's anti-corruption campaign in 2014, this stability maintenance system has been further enhanced and expanded. Xi continues to emphasize the importance of political stability by advocating for a comprehensive view of national security. He calls for integrated planning that accounts for both development and national security.

3.1.2 Taxation Strategies of the Central Government

As shown in what follows, the Chinese central government has developed several strategies to balance the trilemma of policy objectives. We detail the evolution and tradeoffs of these strategies in turn.

Centralization of Legislative Power in Taxation. Under China's one-party regime, the CCP Central Committee, the National People's Congress (NPC) and its Standing Committee (NPCSC), and the State Council wield the ultimate legislative power necessary to promulgate laws and regulations for taxation;

---

[31] Mao Zedong (1991 [1942]), "Economic and financial problems during the Anti-Japanese War" (1991: 891).

and they could override those made by the subnational legislatures.[32] China's governance structure has undergone several centralization–decentralization cycles since 1949 as did the degree and form of taxation power.

In 1950, the newly established Government Administration Council of the Central Government of China (replaced by the State Council in 1954) issued the *Decision on the Unifying National Tax Administration*. This directive required that prefectural and county governments obtain provincial approval for tax legislation while provincial tax policies required authorization from the central government.[33] The tax legislation power was then decentralized from 1958 to 1970, offering provincial governments greater autonomy in making tax policy. In 1977, however, the Chinese central government recentralized the tax legislation power, when the State Council approved the MOF's *Request for Instruction on the Tax Administration System* (Editorial board of *Contemporary China Finance* 1990). This move became a new starting point for subsequent tax reforms in 1980s and 1990s (Cui 2012; Zhang 2018: 20–21, 60–64).

Specifically, the State Council maintained greater autonomy in tax policy-making. For instance, the NPC delegated tax legislative power to the State Council in 1984, allowing the latter to create bylaws, regulations, and temporary or transitional measures related to taxation without engaging in the legislative process at the NPC. Even the 1994 TSS reform bypassed the NPC or NPCSC: It was approved only by the CCP Central Committee and the State Council. The only exceptions in tax legislation were those related to foreign individuals and entities, such as the PIT (initially targeting foreigners in the early 1980s) and the foreign enterprise income tax law.

The NPC and the State Council possess the legislative authority to introduce new taxes, reform existing ones, and restructure the tax system to broaden the tax base and enhance its rationality. Through these measures, they seek to strengthen fiscal capacity and advance the development of a socialist market economy. Notably, despite the centralization of legislative power in taxation, the tax administration is highly decentralized because of China's vast size and uneven development. The central government can enact tax policies as it sees fit with the full understanding that the enforcement of these laws and policies depends heavily on the efforts of local governments, which hold significant discretionary power in policy implementation, a realm lying beyond the central government's full control. Hence, the central government must ensure that

---

[32] See O'Brien (1990) and Tanner (1995) for China's lawmaking process and the evolution of the National People's Congress.
[33] "State Council's Decision on Unifying the State's Financial and Economic Work" from the editorial board of *Contemporary China Finance* (1990).

when making tax policy, the incentive structure of local governments is considered in its implementation.

Institutionalization of Taxation to Stimulate Economic Growth. A well-functioning market economy – where market prices serve as key signals for business operations – is essential for fiscal policies to effectively serve as instruments for microeconomic management. As China transitioned to a market economy after 1992, fiscal policies were increasingly designed to fulfill this purpose (Huang 1996; Yang 2020: 6–9). Specifically, tax and fee reduction (TFR) has been a primary instrument to stimulate economic growth since 2008. Initially, the Chinese government called it "structural tax reduction," associated with tax and fee reform and "universal tax deduction." Furthermore, the Chinese government shifted from a proactive expansionary fiscal policy to TFR for the purpose of stimulating economic growth since 2015, resembling a fundamental part of supply-side structural reform.

Tax and fee reduction has frequently appeared in government work reports and the formulation of macroeconomic policies since 2008 (see Table 2 for a list of these policies). For instance, the VAT reform (including BT-to-VAT reform) was announced to stimulate businesses, and the PIT reform was intended to stimulate domestic consumption. In addition, the central government launched

Table 2 Tax and fee deduction policies

Tax reduction		Reduce tax rates: VAT reform, BT-to-VAT reform (2016), PIT reform (2018)
		Reduce tax base: 25% deduction for income tax of micro and small enterprises; deduction or exemption from vehicle purchase tax
		Tax exemption: for nonprofit organizations, individual income tax reform
		Tax credit: tax deduction for donations
		Tax moratorium: for micro, small, and medium-sized manufacturing enterprises
		Tax refund: VAT credit refund
Fee reduction	Social security	Reduce rates for pension, unemployment insurance, and employment injury insurance (2019)
	Administrative fee	Reduce some specific fees (2019)
	Government fund	Reduce disabled persons' employment security fund and others (2018)

a wide range of policies to support small and micro enterprises, venture capital investment, and technological innovation. Between 2012 and 2017, the BT-to-VAT reform reduced an estimated 2 trillion yuan in tax burdens, and other tax and fee deduction policies reduced the equivalent of another 1 trillion. In 2018, an estimated 800 billion in tax deductions and 300 billion in fee deductions occurred (Zhang and Yang 2020: 224). Now it covers the process of production, investment, consumption, and innovation.

3.2 Local Government Challenge: Fulfilling Competing Mandates

Local governments serve as agents of the central government under China's unitary political system. To entice compliance from local governments, the CCP has established a nomenklatura system operating as a pressure-based system (see Section 2.3.2). Although they share many policy goals with central authorities, they face competing and sometimes conflicting mandates from higher-level government. Hence, local politicians strive to selectively fulfill these policy targets, particularly those quantitatively measurable (O'Brien and Li 1999).

Collecting tax revenues has consistently ranked among the most crucial indicators in the evaluation of local officials. The primacy of taxation in cadre evaluation is twofold. First, given that officials tend to manipulate GDP data, tax revenue serves as a more reliable indicator of local officials' performance (Lü and Landry 2014). Second, greater tax revenue enables local government to finance local public spending, from urban development to local public goods provision, crucial to fulfill the unfunded mandates from the central government (Wong and Bird 2008). The 1994 TSS reform expanded expenditure obligations for local governments while shrinking their share of tax revenue; therefore, raising tax revenues became an imperative for local governments. In the following sections, we first provide a brief overview of local governments' objectives regarding taxation within the framework of the cadre management system, then explore how local governments use taxation to meet policy targets set by higher-level authorities.

3.2.1 Objectives of Local Governments

By and large, local governments prioritize four policy areas: promoting regional economic growth, fulfilling the taxation revenue quotas, financing local public spending, and maintaining local stability.

Economic Growth. Economic growth became a primary policy objective after CCP leaders shifted their top priority from class struggle to economic development and pursuit of the "four modernizations" (四个现代化) in 1978.

Consequently, the political selection of local politicians has been increasingly based on local economic performance, not simply ideological conformity or personal ties. Some scholars argue that local politicians participate in a "promotion tournament," in which those who achieve better GDP growth rates in their jurisdictions are rewarded with promotions (Li and Zhou 2005; Yao and Zhang 2015). By tying cadre promotion to economic growth, the central government creates strong incentives for local politicians to engage in economic development, explaining China's rapid growth in the last three decades.

Fulfilling Quotas for Taxation Revenue. The quota system for tax revenue, a remnant of the planned economy, involved higher-level governments setting quotas for tax revenues for remission by lower-level governments (see Section 2.3.2 for more detail). This practice persisted into the fiscal contracting system of the 1980s, where lower-level governments signed tax contracts with higher-level authorities, specifying tax quotas and annual growth rates.

The typical practice of the tax quota entails the following steps. At the beginning of a year, usually around the time of the NPC Annual Meeting in March, the central government officially announced the targets for annual GDP growth rate and fiscal revenue. Once the total fiscal revenue target was established, it was distributed among lower-level governments. Local governments meeting or exceeding their tax revenue targets were rewarded both economically (through bonuses) and politically (with better promotion prospects). No standardized procedure or scientific method was in place for setting these targets; instead, they reflected the preferences of party–government leaders (Cui 2022; Zhang 2021).

Financing Local Public Spending. Economic growth is not the only source for the Chinese government's performance legitimacy. The expansion of public goods provision is another way to enhance its popular support. Since 2002 under the Hu–Wen regime, the CCP responded to rising social discontent by expanding social spending. For instance, the Chinese central government launched several initiatives to expand public goods provision in both rural and urban China in the 2010s, including the abolition of compulsory school tuition and fees (Lü 2014) and the expansion of rural healthcare and pension system (Huang 2014) as well as the institution of the social protection program (Huang 2020; Pan 2020). Although the central government has established various intergovernmental transfers to assist local governments in financing these policy initiatives, local governments bear responsibility for covering most expenses.[34] Consequently, local governments face mounting pressure to identify fiscal resources to fund these mandates from higher-level governments.

---

[34] See Lü (2015) for the case of intergovernmental transfers and local education spending.

Maintaining Local Stability. Promoting rapid economic growth can be costly. Chinese society has experienced rising social contention since the 1990s, driven by a wide range of issues like SOE reform, rural governance, labor conflict, government land expropriation, and environmental degradation.[35] Since 2008, stability maintenance has become a crucial criterion for evaluating local governments' performance, especially at the county and township level. Because those in higher-level governments view stability maintenance as a veto issue and citizens recognize that grassroots governments may make concessions, maintaining stability has increasingly become an expensive endeavor, consuming a substantial portion of local expenditures.[36] Not only do local governments use social spending to mitigate potential social unrest, but they also sometimes outsource coercion to nonstate actors in order to quell social contention from citizens (Ong 2022).

3.2.2 Taxation Strategies of Local Governments

The previous section underscores how local governments must navigate a range of competing mandates from higher-level governments, requiring them to balance their efforts across multiple goals. Their tax collection strategies are primarily influenced by two key factors. First, the degree of political competition for promotion shapes local politicians' intensity in tax collection. Second, competing mandates compel local governments to exercise their discretionary authority in policy implementation, either offering tax incentives or adopting aggressive tax collection practices.

Interjurisdiction Competition and Tax Collection. Scholars have attributed China's success in promoting economic growth to regionally decentralized authoritarianism (RDA), characterized by highly centralized political powers and high-decentralized administrative and economic powers (Jin, Qian, and Weingast 2005; Landry 2008; Montinola, Qian, and Weingast 1995; Xu 2011). Under RDA, local politicians are incentivized to engage in interjurisdictional competition in the realm of economic development and fiscal extraction to enhance prospects for their promotion (Jia, Kudamatsu, and Seim 2015; Landry, Lü, and Duan 2018; Li and Zhou 2005).

Most local officials actively seek promotion but do not always maximize tax revenue in this endeavor: Not only does an onerous tax burden hinder economic growth, but it could also undermine the political stability valued by higher-level governments. Furthermore, the level of fiscal revenue is not only determined by local officials' efforts but also by local economic endowments (e.g., geographic

---

[35] See Ong and Göbel (2014) for a review of social unrest in China.
[36] See Lee and Zhang (2013) and Pan (2020) for "buying" stability.

locations, human capital accumulation, and natural resources), and sometimes luck (e.g., external economic booms and crises, natural disasters). Consequently, local officials may exert varying degrees of effort in tax collection. Lü and Landry (2014) present a theoretical framework undergirding the logic of interjurisdictional political competition and fiscal extraction in China, proposing an inverted U-shaped relationship between the intensity of political competition and fiscal revenue. The intuition behind this framework is that local politicians exert minimal effort when political competition is either too intense or too weak as fiscal revenue becomes less pivotal in both scenarios.

Discretionary Power of Local Governments. Given the competing mandates imposed by higher-level governments, local politicians employ diverse tax strategies to navigate these pressing needs. Specifically, although local governments have no legislative power to set tax rates or change tax policies, they wield considerable discretion in implementing tax policies; therefore, local governments concurrently employ strategies of generous tax rebates and predatory tax collection.

The tax target system incentivizes local governments to use their discretionary power to adjust actual tax remittances, driven by a fear of the ratchet effect. On one hand, local governments in economically prosperous regions often adopt strategic tax collection practices when facing substantial revenue surplus over the tax target. Instead of strictly enforcing full tax collection, they collect just enough to exceed the target, allowing enterprises to retain the surplus, an approach effectively creating a financial cushion for more challenging times (Chen and Zhang 2021; Zhang 2021). On the other hand, local governments lacking the fiscal capacity to create tax reservoirs must resort to various tactics to meet the target set by higher-level authorities, particularly during economic downturns. For instance, some local governments collect future tax revenues (预征税款) or temporarily lend to taxpayers (税收空转). Others go as far as borrowing funds from local banks to meet tax targets (借款交税) or purchasing tax revenue (买税) from other jurisdictions (Tan and Zhao 2008; Zhang 2021). In some cases, particularly in rural areas, scholars have observed predatory and even violent methods employed by local governments during the tax collection process (Bernstein and Lü 2003).

Meanwhile, many local governments often offer tax breaks to local firms because they faced intensive regional tax competition to promote economic growth in the 1990s and 2000s. These local governments employed legal and illegal tax breaks in the form of tax deductions and tax rebates associated with preferential industrial and land policies to attract external investments (Chen and Zhang 2021; Pearson, Rithmire, and Tsai 2023; Whiting 2001). This practice leads to a race to the bottom in tax collection, creating an adverse impact, including damaging the business environment, disturbing market order, undermining tax revenue, and distorting competition among enterprises.

One rationale for local governments providing tax breaks is that China's nominal tax rates are often set at levels too high for strict enforcement. During the early period of tax reform, the Chinese central government intentionally sets high tax rates to help the newly established tax bureaus meet the tax target, given the inadequate tax administration capacity in 1994. Nevertheless, the significant expansion of taxation capacity in subsequent years rendered these rates too high for most firms despite several rounds of adjustment. The de facto tax burden is further exacerbated after considering the social security contribution made by firms; consequently, offering tax breaks remains a routine practice of many local governments (Zhang 2021).

3.3 Tax Reforms and the Trilemma

Although the central government holds the ultimate authority in the design and legislation of tax policies, local governments possess the discretionary power to shape the implementation of policies to serve their own interests. This dynamic is on full display in the cycles of centralization–decentralization in various tax reforms initiated by the central government facing the trilemma. When the central government launches one policy reform to achieve a particular policy goal, local governments' responses inadvertently generate a series of unintended consequences undermining other policy goals, forcing the former to adjust its policy orientation and adopt another reform years later. The strategic interactions of the central and local governments offer a crucial lens for examining the two major tax reforms of the 1980s and 1990s: The fiscal contracting system[37] and the 1994 TSS reform as well as other reforms, including the abolition of rural taxation and the reform of enterprise tax, VAT, and PIT. Wong (2018: 273) describes the process of fiscal reform as "incremental and reactive, aimed principally at 'putting out fires.'"

3.3.1 Fiscal Contracting System

Facing economic stagnation due to a rigidly planned economy and the over-centralized "unitary remittance and unitary expenditure" (统收统支) fiscal system in the 1970s, the central government gradually decentralized taxation and expenditure power in the early 1980s to stimulate economic growth. The primary objective of the so-called fiscal contracting system (财政包干制 or 分灶吃饭, "eating from separate stoves") was to offer local governments greater

---

[37] See Wong (1991).

autonomy in pursuing tailored strategies to develop their regional economies. Each level of local government entered fiscal contracts with their respective higher-level governments, committing to remit a specified amount of tax revenue while retaining all or a substantial portion of any surplus. One distinct feature of the fiscal contracting system is that local governments were bound to individualized contracts, negotiated individually with higher authorities and subject to renegotiation every one to three years.

The tax reform under the fiscal contracting system entailed several steps. On February 1, 1980, the State Council issued a document titled "Tentative Provisions on Implementing the Financial Management System for Dividing Revenue and Expenditure and Contracting Responsibilities at Various Levels [关于实行划分收支、分级包干财政管理体制的暂行规定]," which led to a major fiscal system transition. From 1980 to 1983, the central government focused on merging tax categories and simplifying tax collection while maintaining the same level of tax obligations on local governments. The goals were twofold: Maintaining revenue growth throughout the transition to the market economy and accommodating new economic activities and economic sectors emerging in rural areas. In 1984 the central government turned its attention to urban China, initiating the tax-for-profit (利改税) reform with more ambitious goals, including "promoting the reform of the urban economic system, further invigorating the economy, adjusting and improving the distribution relationship between the state and enterprises, and incentivizing enterprises and workers."[38] Under this reform, SOEs paid taxes instead of profit remittance to the government. Furthermore, the central government introduced several new taxes in 1984: Corporation income tax, merchandise tax, VAT, BT, SOE income tax, and SOE adjustment tax. These taxes were designed to replace SOE profit remittance incrementally as part of SOE reform, especially to separate SOEs from the government. Unsurprisingly, SOE profit remittance and its share of fiscal income decreased steadily thereafter (Figure 6). Figure 9 illustrates the major tax reforms and the price and salary system reforms initiated by the central government to dismantle the planned economy and promote economic growth.

The 1980s fiscal and economic decentralization was crucial to China's economic success, signaling the CCP's credible commitment to growth and incentivizing local governments and firms to boost economic activities (Oi 1992; Qian and Weingast 1997). Nonetheless, the fiscal contracting system generated several unintended consequences. For instance, separating SOEs

---

[38] The Ministry of Finance, "Trial Measures on the Second Step of SOEs' Tax-for-Profit Reform," August 10, 1984. *Editorial Board of Contemporary China's Finance* (1990): 823.

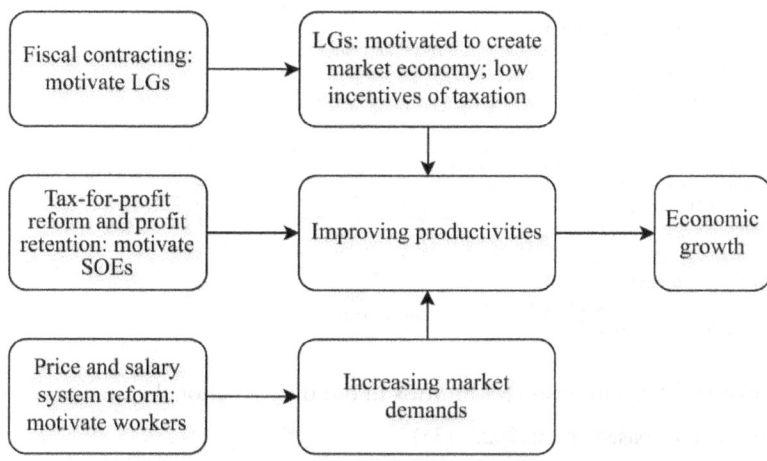

Figure 9 Fiscal contracting reform (1980–1993).

Note: Modified based on Lü (2022: 93). LG stands for local government.

from the government proved to be more challenging; thus a hard budgetary constraint was imposed on SOEs (Qian and Roland 1998; Qian and Xu 1998). Specific contracting between the central government and local governments created a fragmented market, in which local governments set high trade barriers against one another (诸侯经济). In addition, the share of fiscal revenue obtained by the central government persistently declined throughout the 1980s. These unintended consequences reflect the trilemma faced by the central government because the promotion of economic growth undermined the central government's fiscal capacity.

3.3.2 1994 Tax-Sharing System Reform

To address the issues stemming from the 1980s fiscal and economic decentralization, the central government initiated the 1994 TSS reform. Its launch became possible after CCP leaders cleared critical obstacles and reached a consensus, a feat they were unable to accomplish in the 1980s because of resistance from provincial leaders and Deng's ambivalence (Jin and Chen 2005; Liu and Jia 2008). During the aftermath of the 1989 student movement, conservative CCP leaders gained the upper hand in resisting comprehensive economic reform. Deng Xiaoping, however, strategically maneuvered the conflicting elite interests and endorsed a broader economic reform after his signature 1992 southern tour (Vogel 2011). In November 1993, the CCP's Third Plenary Session of 14th Central Committee passed "The Resolution of the CCP Central Committee on Some Issues Concerning the Establishment of

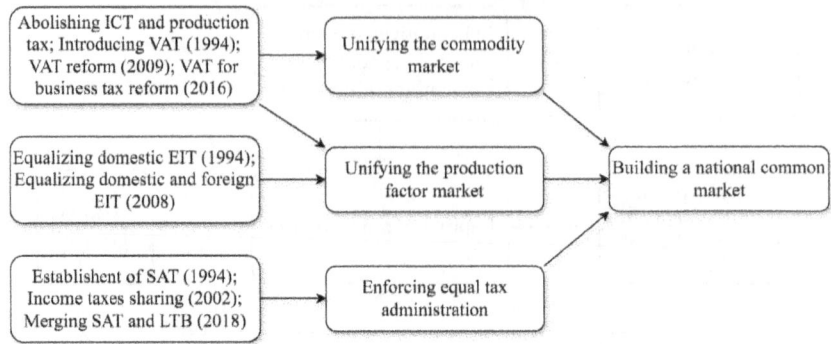

Figure 10 TSS and post-TSS reforms in building a national common market
Note: Modified based on Lü (2022: 136).

the Socialist Market Economy System," stating the inseparability of the socialist market economy system from the basic socialist system (Academic Affairs Division of the CCP Central Party School, 2015: 218–234). Facing a determined Politburo Standing Committee supported by party elders, provincial leaders had little room to resist the TSS reform; nonetheless, their governments negotiated with Premier Zhu Rongji and the Ministry of Finance officials for some "technical" issues, including tax rates, revenue baselines for tax sharing, and intergovernmental transfers.[39]

The central government launched these tax reforms in its effort to build a national common market to further economic reform while retaining a greater share of revenue collection (Figure 10). Under TSS reform, the central government retains fiscal revenues from sources including customs and associated VAT, and consumption taxes as well as income taxes from centrally controlled SOEs and the finance sector. Local governments retain fiscal revenues from sources like business tax, income tax from locally controlled SOEs, and PIT; central and local governments share tax revenues from VAT, natural resource tax, and stock transaction taxes. The 1994 TSS reform designated 75% of the VAT to the central government, with 25% to local governments. The TSS reform successfully transformed the central-local fiscal relations, as the central government now retains approximately 60% of the total fiscal revenue while decentralizing many spending obligations to local governments.[40] When the

---

[39] Liu and Jia (2008) present some evidence based on memoirs of the reform and central–local bargaining.
[40] See Wong and Bird (2008) and Lin (2022) for the specific arrangements. Liu, Martinez-Vazquez, and Wu (2017) offer the empirical evidence evaluating the impact of this reform on regional inequality in China.

central government replaced industry and commerce taxes (ICT) and production tax with VAT in 1994, the latter helped reduce trade barriers for commodities and production and the local governments' incentive for regional protectionism. In addition, the central government leveled the playing field by equalizing enterprise income tax (EIT) among firms with different ownership types in 1994 and 2008, unifying the production factor market and providing equal competition among firms. Finally, the central government established an independent and vertically managed SAT alongside the LTB in 1994, aiming to curb local governments' race to the bottom in attracting investment through de facto tax rates.

Liu et al. (2022) contend that the TSS reform wasn't unidimensional – the intent was to rein in inflation and tighten the monetary supply. They call it a grand bargain: Along with the 1994 TSS, "the central government was simultaneously giving localities new autonomy and resources to obtain their own funds in order to achieve the regions' cooperation with the fiscal and later financial recentralization" (45). Provincial governments, therefore, obtained the autonomy to establish commercial banks and a regional land market, later becoming the institutional foundation for local governments' investment-driven growth model and leading to the serious local government debt problems discussed in Session 5.[41] Notably, the 1994 TSS imposed tremendous pressure on local governments to raise the necessary fiscal revenue for public expenditures because of the centralization of revenue and decentralization of spending obligations. County and township governments faced the greatest challenges in revenue collection and public expenditure, thereby straining state–society relations in rural China in the years to come.

3.3.3 Agricultural Tax Reform

The 1994 TSS reform heightened the demand for fiscal extraction, leading to predatory and excessive tax collection practices by local governments, particularly at the county and township levels. In many regions, especially in central China, peasants bore significant tax burdens, with some impoverished households dedicating over 30% of their annual income to taxes and fees (Tao et al. 2003: 5). This heavy financial strain fueled growing social discontent within rural communities, undermining CCP legitimacy. In other words, TSS reform bolstered the central government's fiscal capacity and advanced economic reform but at the cost of local stability.

---

[41] Given all these concessions, Liu et al. (2022) even argue that the TSS reform was a de jure centralization but a de facto centralization.

Gradually, the Chinese central government came to recognize the need for an agricultural tax reform to alleviate the peasant burden and improve state–peasant relations. Facing a weak elite coalition in the CCP Politburo, the Hu–Wen administration pivoted toward bolstering mass support as a form of populist authoritarianism (Tang 2016). The agricultural tax reform was an economical option, given that agricultural taxes contributed only 2.38% of the total tax revenue by 2000. Furthermore, agricultural tax reform could serve as a strategy to discipline exploitative township and village cadres by depriving them of the power they wielded through predatory tax collection (Li and Zhang 2025).

The central government piloted the tax-for-fee reform (费改税) in Anhui province in 2000 and Jiangsu in 2001, eventually abolishing agricultural taxes and fees in 2006.[42] To compensate for the budgetary shortfall stemming from the agricultural tax reform, the central government initiated various fiscal transfers, including those for agricultural taxes and fees reform, rural education, and grassroots fiscal deficits. Consequently, many local governments lost their autonomy and became more fiscally dependent on higher-level governments (Oi et al. 2012). Moreover, the abolition of agricultural taxes undercut grassroots cadres' incentives to implement unpopular state policies, further fueling mass petitions and protests in rural China (Hou, Liu, and Lü 2024).

3.3.4 VAT and Enterprise Tax Reforms

BT-to-VAT (营改增) reform was perhaps the most significant tax reform since the 1994 TSS reform. After three decades of rapid economic growth, China became the world's second-largest economy in 2010. Sustaining this growth has become increasingly challenging, and rapid growth has generated a negative impact on the environment. These concerns prompted the central government to consider upgrading its economic structure and reducing its heavy reliance on manufacturing. One central government strategy is to reshape firms' incentives through tax reforms. Under the 1994 TSS reform, firms operating in the manufacturing and industrial sectors were subject to the VAT, but firms in the service sector fell under the BT. This dual tax system put firms in the service sector at a disadvantage because they shared the tax burden stemming from a form of revenue-based VAT across supply chains, but they were unable to benefit from tax deductions related to VAT, which is regarded as a price-distorting cascading tax (Cui 2014). As the service sector became a major pillar of the Chinese economy, the central government launched the BT-to-VAT reform, intending to replace the price-distorting BT with a more economically

---

[42] See Göbel (2010) for the origins of the agricultural tax reform and its procedures.

efficient VAT in the service sector. Piloted in Shanghai in January 2012, BT-to-VAT reform was implemented gradually. By May 2016 the reform was fully implemented across all service sectors nationwide, marking the beginning of the new VAT system in China.

The Chinese central government considered the BT-to-VAT reform part of supply-side reform (供给侧改革), with an overall goal to restructure the Chinese economy from labor-intensive manufacturing to service-oriented by easing the tax burden on the service sector. To this end, BT-to-VAT reform was designed to rationalize the tax system by reducing repetitive taxing and alleviating businesses' tax burdens and to encourage low-end manufacturers to upgrade their technology by investing in R&D (Gao 2013). Prior to BT-to-VAT reform, the VAT was collected by local offices of the SAT, and VAT revenue was shared between central (75%) and local governments (25%). Meanwhile, BT was a form of local tax collected by LTB. To compensate for the loss of revenue by local governments, the new VAT was equally shared by the central (50%) and local governments (50%). BT-to-VAT reform accelerated the consolidation of the SAT and LTB in 2018 and also raised the question of how to create sufficient tax sources for local governments.

Although BT-to-VAT reform aimed to alleviate firms' tax burdens, its actual impact hinged on the interplay between adjusted tax rates and the effectiveness of the VAT deduction chain. Notably, the reform reduced the share of taxes on goods and services from nearly 60% in 1999 to 40% in 2021, ultimately weakening the state's fiscal capacity.

3.3.5 Personal Income Tax Reform

The Third Session of the Fifth NPC promulgated the first Personal Income Tax Law of the People's Republic of China in 1980. The economic growth has generated greater inequality in China since the 1980s, making it one of the most unequal countries in the world (Knight 2013; Xie and Zhou 2014). Concerned about the possible backlash against regime legitimacy and political stability, the Chinese government has attempted to alleviate potential tension by cutting PITs since the mid-2010s. Most of these early PIT reforms centered on the revision of the PIT exemption threshold. The 2018 PIT reform, implemented in 2019, was the most comprehensive. In its public announcement, the Chinese government stated that "the purpose of the 2018 PIT reform is to further facilitate, benefit, and bring favors to the people (便民、利民、惠民)."[43] Liu Shangxi, the Dean

---

[43] Shanghai Municipal Tax Service, State Taxation Administration, "Explain the New Personal Income Tax Law Transition Period: Hot Policy Questions." https://shanghai.chinatax.gov.cn/qptax/ztzl/gsggzl/201810/t442138.html (last access August 27, 2024).

of the MOF's Academy of Fiscal Sciences, summarizes the purposes of the 2018 PIT reform as "reducing [the] tax burden for middle-and-low-income citizens while improving fair taxation and [the] tax's redistributive effects."[44] These PIT reforms, especially the one in 2018, not only embodied populist authoritarianism – the motivation of Chinese leaders – but also aimed to enhance the legibility capacity of China's tax bureaucracy (see Section 4.1.1 for details).

As demonstrated in Section 5.1.1, PIT reform inadvertently heightened the salience of personal income tax in China. The CCP Central Committee announced the need to strengthen the administrative capacity for direct taxation as one of the priorities for future tax reforms in China in the Third Plenary Session of its 20th Central Committee on July 18, 2024. Specifically, the CCP Central Committee announced its intention to "establish a sound direct tax system; improve the comprehensive and categorized PIT system; standardize tax policies for business income, capital gains, and property income; and implement unified taxation for labor income" in 2024. The effects of this policy shift remain to be seen.

3.4 Conclusion

After several rounds of tax reforms, China's tax system has been significantly rationalized, but notable deficiencies remain. One of the major challenges comprises insufficient tax revenue sources for local governments, a problem that intensified following the BT-to-VAT reform and the decline in land transfer fees due to recent economic downturns. Addressing the need to build a robust tax system for local governments has become a critical topic for future reforms; however, increasing local governments' share of the VAT or enterprise income tax is not a viable solution because it would exacerbate tax competition among local governments (Zhu 2014). Similarly, property tax is not an ideal option either, given the sharp rise in housing prices and the current decline in the real estate industry.

Despite challenges in revenue collection to meet rising public spending demands, the Chinese government has implemented several tax reduction measures over the past decades, including abolishing agricultural taxes and narrowing the scope of PIT. These reforms are puzzling because taxation has not been the primary source of tension in state–society relations, particularly in urban China. In the next two sections, we explore the political attitudes and

---

[44] *Xinhua*, "Experts are Hot Talking about a Tax Law Amendment: Strengthening the Anti-Tax Avoidance Power of Tax Authorities," news.sina.com.cn/o/2018–06–19/doc-iheauxvz7742919.shtml (last access August 27, 2024).

behaviors of citizens and businesses in response to tax policies. Drawing on diverse data sources, we illustrate reasons that the Chinese government remains highly cautious about potential backlash from fiscal extraction – concerns that are well founded.

4 Taxation and State–Society Relations: Perspectives from Citizens and Business

Thus far, we have concentrated on the "supply side" of taxation in China, examining efforts by central and local governments to raise fiscal revenue and address challenges arising from their tax policies. In this section, we shift our focus to the "demand side," exploring the political behaviors of Chinese citizens and businesses in response to tax policies.

Historically and contemporarily, taxation has been a focal point of state–society conflict, shaping political attitudes and inciting protests and even revolts across societies. Taxation appears to be somewhat limited in generating state–society conflict in cotemporary China, perhaps except for rural taxation. The obscure nature of the effect of taxation on state–society relations in China is partly driven by the structure of fiscal revenue and tax collection, mitigating societal conflict stemming from taxation (Zhang 2021; Zhang and Dickson 2024). Specifically, the Chinese half-tax state has relied on indirect taxation and nontax revenue for fiscal revenue. In contrast to most developed economies, direct taxation from PIT and rural taxation constitutes only a slim share of the Chinese government's overall fiscal revenue. By 2002, when the Chinese government phased out agriculture taxes and fees, they amounted to only 2.6% of total government tax revenue (Wang and Shen 2014). Meanwhile, PIT has been hovering between 4% and 8% of total government tax revenue since the 1990s (see Figure 5 in Section 2).

If taxation is an inconsequential issue in shaping state–society relations in China, the intense public discourse surrounding tax policies is puzzling. For example, the thresholds for income tax and the expansion of property tax attracted intense media coverage and ignited vibrant debates among Chinese citizens. Furthermore, the seemingly political insignificance of taxation fails to explain why the Chinese government under Xi Jinping has radically shifted its tax policies since 2012 by initiating a series of tax cuts for both businesses and individuals.[45] These tax reduction efforts are even more puzzling given the recent rising government debt since the 2010s resulting from slowing revenue intake.

---

[45] See Section 3 for information on the personal income tax reform and Cui (2022) for a discussion of tax policies under Xi.

To elucidate the enigmatic reversal of the Chinese government's tax policies in the 2010s, we survey existing scholarship as well as survey evidence on taxation and its influence on political behavior in Section 4, arriving at two key observations. First, we find that Chinese urban and rural residents have distinct political attitudes toward taxation. Urbanites tend to have higher tax morale but are very sensitive to tax expansion; furthermore, they hold high expectations of the government in the provision of public goods and services in exchange for taxation. Rural residents, however, have a clearer understanding of their tax burden largely because their obligations take the form of direct taxes compared to their urban counterparts. Earlier scholars attribute the rising rural unrest in the 1990s to the peasant tax burden, but empirical evidence on rural unrest remains contested: Was taxation the primary driver of peasant collective action or merely a pretext for broader grievances regarding poor rural governance?

Second, although firms shoulder over 90% of government tax revenue, they pursue atomized strategies to lower their tax burden or secure preferential treatment rather than building coalitions to influence tax policies. The absence of political action by firms is partly driven by two factors. First, the Chinese political system prevents any organizations from orchestrating broad-based mobilization and coalition building to challenge the state; consequently, Chinese businesses are constrained in organizing political initiatives centered on tax issues. Second, a large share of firms' tax burden comes from indirect taxation (e.g., VAT, business tax); therefore, firms can alleviate their "pain" by simply shifting the tax burden to consumers instead of taking any political action.

In the remainder of Section 4, we first examine existing findings on individual attitudes and behaviors in response to taxation. We then survey studies of state–business relations, focusing on firm behavior driven by taxation. Finally, we conclude by highlighting the most prominent political behaviors Chinese citizens and firms exhibit in response to state tax policies.

4.1 Taxation and Mass Political Behavior

To begin, citizen awareness of the presence and magnitude of the tax burden is the prerequisite for any meaningful impact of taxation on political behavior. Indirect taxation, exemplified by VAT and sales tax, is often considered a form of "hidden tax" because it lacks high visibility for consumers. In contrast, direct taxation on income, property, and inheritance, stands as a salient form of taxes crucial to citizen perception. Thus, we investigate the impact of direct taxation on mass political behaviors, assessing them by studying rural and urban populations separately because they are subject to different types of direct taxation.

Chinese urban and rural residents have borne distinct types of direct taxation since the 1980s: Urbanites are subject to PIT and social security contributions, whereas rural residents face agricultural taxes and local government fees. Many if not most urbanites are exempt from income tax because their earnings fall below the thresholds of PIT. Meanwhile, high-income earners employ various strategies for tax avoidance because the Chinese government has not intensified building the bureaucratic infrastructure to tax wealth and capital gains. Hence, individuals in the lower- and middle-income brackets, whose primary incomes come from salaries, carry the most weight of direct taxation because of automatic deductions from their monthly salaries. In contrast, rural households have limited opportunities for tax exemption to circumvent agricultural tax and government fees, making them prominent issues in their interactions with local governments.

4.1.1 Taxation and the Political Behavior of Urbanite

For direct taxation to attain prominence as a political concern, it must first emerge as a notable financial burden or an equity issue. To this end, we first show that the proportion of PIT as a share of the total income of urbanites remains modest; nevertheless, the contribution from social security payments by individual earners has witnessed a growing prominence. On average, the combined share of PIT and social security contributions constitutes 15% to 25% of urbanites' income in 2025.

We then evaluate urbanites' tax morale – whether viewed as a civic duty or as a financial burden. Our examination of several existing public opinion surveys has consistently indicated that most Chinese respondents, especially urbanites, view paying taxes as a civic duty. This finding suggests that the state has successfully framed taxation issues among many citizens. Furthermore, citizens' high tax morale could be driven by their low tax consciousness of the distribution of tax burdens.

Finally, citizen attitudes toward taxation stem from the returns they expect from taxation, such as political accountability as well as public goods and services. The canonical studies of taxation and state building have emphasized a taxation–representation link in taxpayers' fiscal bargaining between the state and the society (Bates and Lien 1985; Levi 1988; North and Weingast 1989). Nevertheless, survey evidence shows that Chinese respondents overwhelmingly prefer public goods and services over the expansion of their political rights in return for their tax payments – except for economic elites. These findings shed light on future political development in China.

Urbanites' Tax Burden. Determining the exact tax burden borne by Chinese urbanites proves elusive because of the absence of publicly available comprehensive administrative data. Instead, researchers on Chinese citizens' tax burden rely on survey data collected by both the National Bureau of Statistics (NBS) and various academic institutions in China. Based on NBS household panel survey data tracking urbanites in sixteen provinces from 1997 to 2009, Xu, Ma, and Li (2013) show that the average effective tax rate rose from 1.12% in 1997 to 3.12% in 2005, then declined to 2.91% in 2009 after the Chinese government raised the exemption threshold of PIT from CNY 800 to CNY 1,600 in 2006. Using the Chinese Household Income Project (CHIP), Xu and Yue (2013) reach a similar conclusion, showing that the average effective individual tax rate was 2.06% in 2002 and 3.27% in 2007. Importantly, they break down the average PIT rate across income deciles, revealing a progressive pattern consistent with the design of China's PIT system. In 2007, for instance, the average tax rate for the bottom decile stood at 0.15%, while the top decile bore a tax burden of 7.74%.

The Chinese government has made several amendments to PIT law since 2005, further raising the exemption threshold of monthly income with each. The latest PIT reform in 2018 elevated the monthly exemption to CNY 5,000 and adjusted the tax brackets. Effectively, the average tax rate for payroll income dropped from 4.8% to 1.9%, and the tax base shrank from 46.7% to 23.4% in China (Zhan, Li, and Xu 2019). The 2018 tax reform was thus a major reduction in PIT for many urbanites.

The shrinking PIT, however, has been replaced by urbanites' other contributions to the state budgets: Social security funds encompassing pension, healthcare, and unemployment benefits as well as the Housing Provident Fund.[46] For instance, the nominal rates for individual social security contributions range from 15% to 23% of personal income; however, the effective personal contributions to these social security funds exhibit substantial variation across regions and among individuals in the same city (Figure 11). The variations stem from two main sources.[47] First, the decentralization of social security funds by the Chinese government to local administrations has resulted in divergent rates of individual contributions across localities, depending on local governments' efforts in managing social security funds. Second, many nonstate employers, especially small private firms, have pursued strategies to evade their portion of social security contributions, some of which (underreporting social security wages) reduce the individual contributions of urbanites to these funds.

---

[46] See Huang (forthcoming) for a comprehensive review of China's social protection system.
[47] See Fang and Feng (2020) and Frazier (2010) for an excellent overview of the state and evolution of China's pension policies since the reform era.

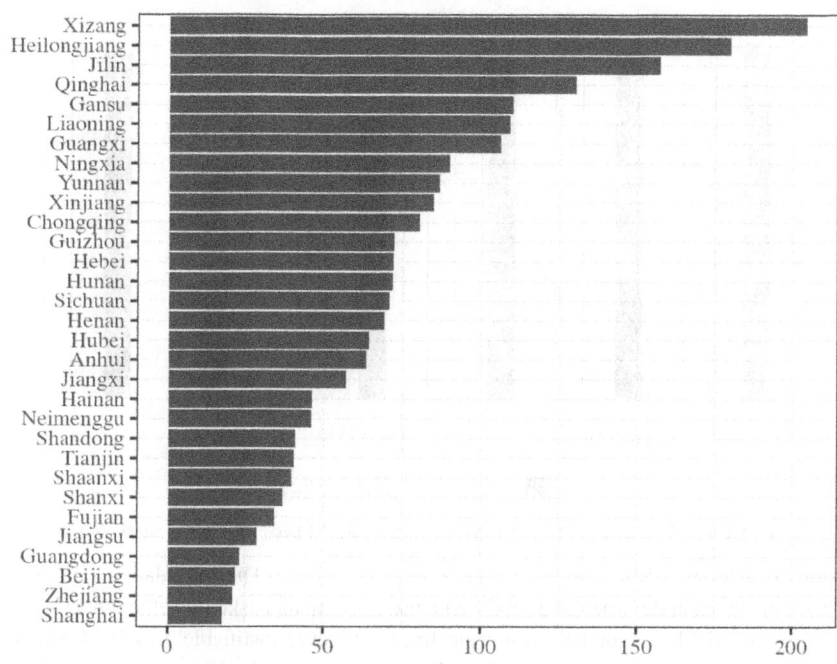

Figure 11 Social security spending to tax ratio by province in 2022.

Note: Data derived from the NBS. Social Security and employment expenditures encompass government spending on various social security and employment-related activities, including management of social security and employment affairs, civil administration, financial subsidies to social insurance funds, contributions to the national social security fund, and retirement provisions for public institutions.

Taxation as a Civic Duty. Several waves of the World Value Survey (WVS) since 1990 included a question on tax morale: Justification for tax evasion.[48] When Chinese respondents were questioned on the justifiability of cheating on taxes, they overwhelmingly rejected this idea, more than 75% of them deeming it never justifiable from 1990 to 2001 (Figure 12); however, tax morale declined significantly in the next decade, when only 58.3% and 43.4% of Chinese respondents expressed this view in the 2007 and 2012 surveys, respectively. The responses bounced back to 77.8% in 2018. Compared to other countries, China's tax morale is unexceptional. In the 2010–2014 wave of the WVS, for instance, greater than 70% of respondents in OECD and Latin

---

[48] WVS is a collaboration among academic institutions around the world to study social, political, economic, religious, and cultural values. See www.worldvaluessurvey.org for more detail.

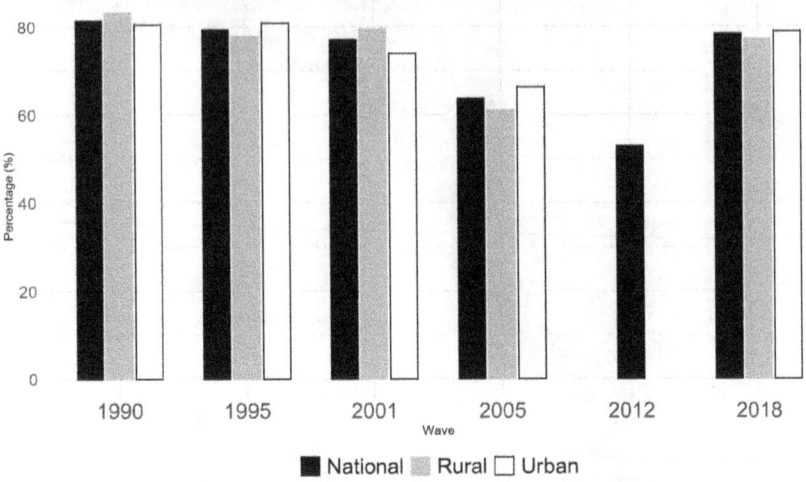

Figure 12 Is cheating on taxes justifiable? (World Value Survey).

Note: This figure is based on WVS data from 1990 to 2018. The 2012 data did not have a variable to separate urban and rural residents. Participants asked whether cheating on taxes is justifiable responded on a scale from 1 ("never justifiable") to 10, ("always justifiable"). We coded "never justifiable" as 1, and zero otherwise, excluding all the respondents who chose either "refuse to answer" or "don't know."

American countries indicated that they could never justify cheating on taxes. In fact, the share of Chinese respondents expressing the same view in 2012 was lower than the average for emerging Asian economies, which stood at approximately 60% (OECD 2019).

Although social desirability bias represents an acute issue in public opinion data collection in authoritarian regimes, this rationale cannot explain the temporal fluctuation observed in responses to this question in China. Furthermore, in the Chinese context, questions about tax morale are relatively less sensitive compared to inquiries regarding the regime or government officials. This distinction suggests that other factors beyond social desirability bias may contribute to observed patterns of tax morale, studies of which have highlighted a host of drivers: Cultural norms, religious beliefs, regime type, institutional quality, and trust in government.[49] Multiple waves of national surveys indicate that Chinese citizens exhibit high levels of trust in government (Li 2016), which may help explain the seemingly high tax morale in

---

[49] Alm and Torgler (2006) produced an early study using cross-national surveys like the WVS to study determinants of tax morale. See Luttmer and Singhal (2014) and OECD (2019) for an overview of this literature.

China. Another alternative explanation may involve the reliance on indirect taxation in China's tax revenue, noted previously: Citizens express high tax morale largely because they are not confronted with the consequences of tax compliance. Figure 12, however, demonstrates that rural respondents – despite facing direct taxation through agricultural taxes and fees – exhibit tax morale resembling their urban counterparts. Thus, reliance on indirect taxation may not be the primary determinant of tax morale in China.

Perception of Tax Burden. The degree of resentment stemming from taxation depends not only on the absolute tax burden but also on relative ones. Both the objective and subjective evaluations of individuals' tax burden significantly shape their attitudes toward taxation.[50] In the case of Chinese urbanites, survey data reveal that they seem to have little knowledge of the distribution of the tax burden across taxpayers.

In a 2014 survey of a national random sample of Chinese urbanites, 57.5% of them chose "don't know" or "refuse to respond" in answer to a question about their relative tax burden compared to people they know.[51] Similarly, 64.2% of the respondents chose "don't know" or "refuse to respond" when asked to assess their tax burden relative to the public goods and services they received. This finding parallels the Afrobarometer Survey (2021), where the proportion of respondents selecting "difficult," "very difficult," or "don't know" for the assessment of their own tax burden ranged from 49.83% to 84%, with most responses clustering around 70%. The low tax consciousness observed here aligns with extensive evidence indicating that consumers often misperceive indirect taxes even in developed economies (Congdon, Kling, and Mullainathan 2009). Taxpayers frequently misjudge their actual tax burden, either underestimating or overestimating it because of poor tax perception.[52]

Importantly, most Chinese taxpayers had limited direct experience paying PIT and VAT until the 2018 PIT reform, further obscuring their perception of tax burden.[53] PIT is typically deducted automatically from monthly paychecks unless taxpayers voluntarily report nonsalary income and pay additional taxes to the state tax bureau. Similarly, VAT is embedded in product prices, making it invisible to the average citizen except for those whose professions involve

---

[50] An innovative experimental study in the United States shows that informing subjects about current income distribution and where their household income falls in this distribution has a sizable impact on their views on inequality and public policy preference (Kuziemko et al. 2015).
[51] See Zhang and Dickson (2024) for more detail about this survey.
[52] See Fochmann et al. (2010) for a review on studies of misconceptions of the tax burden.
[53] See discussion in Section 5 on the ways the 2018 PIT reform inadvertently increased the saliency of direct taxation among urbanites.

reporting VAT to the state for their businesses. In the 2017 Chinese Household Finance Survey, only 12.10% of respondents reported awareness of paying PIT; furthermore, only 5.6% recognized indirect payment of VAT.[54] Zhang and Dickson (2024) posit that the limited dependence on individual taxation in the Chinese government's revenue structure diminishes tax salience among citizens.

Citizen Expectations from Taxation. Citizens' tax morale may be shaped by expectations of fiscal exchange, anticipating government provision of public goods and services in return for tax contributions as demonstrated in other studies (Flores-Macías 2018; OECD 2019). In an online survey of urbanites conducted in 2016 by Kao, Lü, and Queralt (2024), respondents were asked why they think paying taxes is important.[55] A total of 53.46% of respondents believe paying taxes is a citizen's civic duty, followed by 25.22% who consider taxation essential to finance public goods and services (Figure 13). Surprisingly, only 4.97% of respondents consider potential punishment for tax evasion as the key motivation for tax compliance. This response starkly contrasts with economic

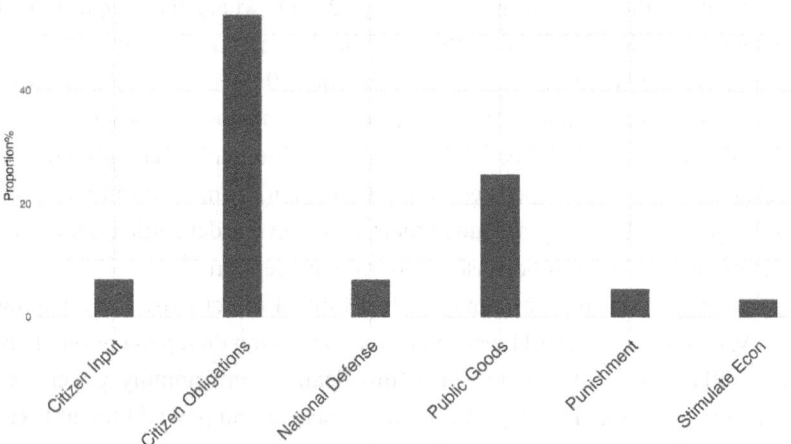

Figure 13 Why is paying taxes important?

Note: Data are based on a 2016 online survey of urban residents conducted by Kao, Lü, and Queralt (2024).

---

[54] The 2017 Chinese Household Finance Survey (中国家庭金融调查) was national representative survey administrated by Southwest University of Finance and Economics. For more details, see their website at https://chfs.swufe.edu.cn/
[55] See the discussion in Kao, Lü, and Queralt (2024) for the design and implementation of this online survey.

theories of tax compliance, which often revolve around the concept of taxpayers engaging in an "audit lottery" to maximize their expected after-tax return, possibly adjusted for their desired level of risk.[56]

In general, Chinese citizens expect the government to provide better public goods and services in return for taxation. Kao, Lü, and Queralt (2024) solicited respondents' preference in return for several types of taxes: Income tax, VAT, and property tax. Figure 14a shows that an overwhelming 60%–80% of the respondents considered public goods and services the important return from taxation. By contrast, citizen input, anti-corruption efforts, and government transparency registered much lower support. This finding is consistent with several waves of the WVS, showing up to 80% of respondents willing to increase taxation to prevent environmental pollution (Figure 14b).

Besides public goods provision, do Chinese citizens view taxation as a tool to mitigate income inequality? Two questions on the 2001 WVS offer a glimpse to this question. In this wave of the survey, Chinese respondents were given two scenarios about the tradeoffs between tax burden and a welfare state: First, "a society with extensive social welfare but high taxes" and second, "a society where taxes are low and individuals take responsibility for themselves." Respondents were then asked to identify which scenario best describes the current state of Chinese society and the direction they believe it should take. Only 25.2% of respondents believe current Chinese society approximates a welfare state with extensive benefits and high taxes (Figure 15a), but 50.8% of respondents stated that such a welfare state is something Chinese society should pursue (Figure 15b). This set of the results is consistent with 2009 and 2014 national surveys focusing on inequality and distributive justice, where close to 70% of respondents preferred progressive income taxation.[57] Notably, Figure 15 reveals the ambivalence of a large share of respondents about these two questions. For example, 34% of respondents cannot determine whether current Chinese society approximates a welfare state or otherwise, and 22% do not know whether China should pursue this type of society. Furthermore, 30% of respondents in the 2009 survey and 20% in the 2014 Social Justice Survey cannot determine whether they prefer progressive income taxation.

Taken together, these survey data reveal two important implications. First, Chinese urbanites exhibit elevated tax morale juxtaposed with low tax consciousness, a phenomenon in part shaped by the marginal role of PIT in overall household earning and the state's propaganda efforts emphasizing taxation as

---

[56] See, for example, Trivedi, Shehata, and Mestelman (2005: 2). See Slemrod (2019) for a review.
[57] The survey was conducted by Marty Whyte, a sociologist from Harvard University. See Whyte (2010) for a detailed discussion of a wide range of results stemming from these surveys.

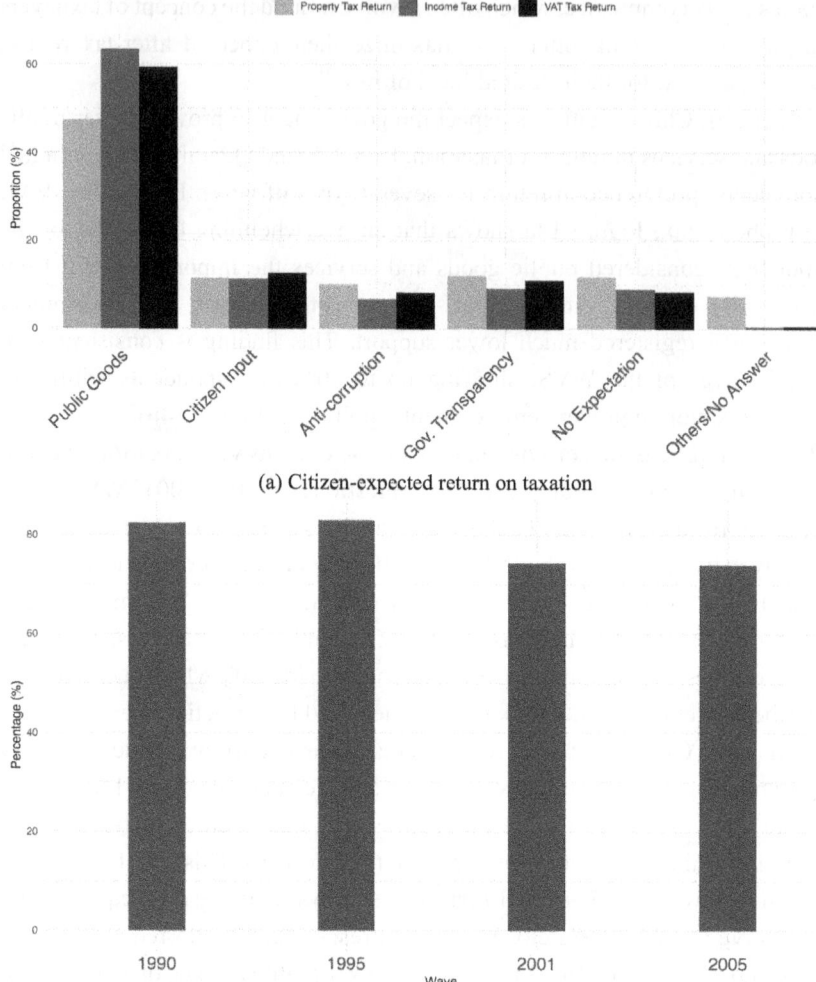

(a) Citizen-expected return on taxation

(b) Willingness to increase taxes to prevent environmental pollution

Figure 14 Taxation and public goods provision

Note: Data for (a) derived from a 2016 online survey of urban residents conducted by Kao, Lü, and Queralt (2024). Figure (b) is based on WVS data from 1990 to 2005. Respondents were asked whether the government can increase taxes if they are used to prevent environmental pollution. Responses ranged from 1 ("strongly agree") to 4 ("strongly disagree"). We coded "strongly agree" and "agree" as 1, and zero otherwise, excluding all respondents choosing "refuse to answer" or "don't know." Finally, we plot the percentage of those who responded either "strongly agree" or "agree."

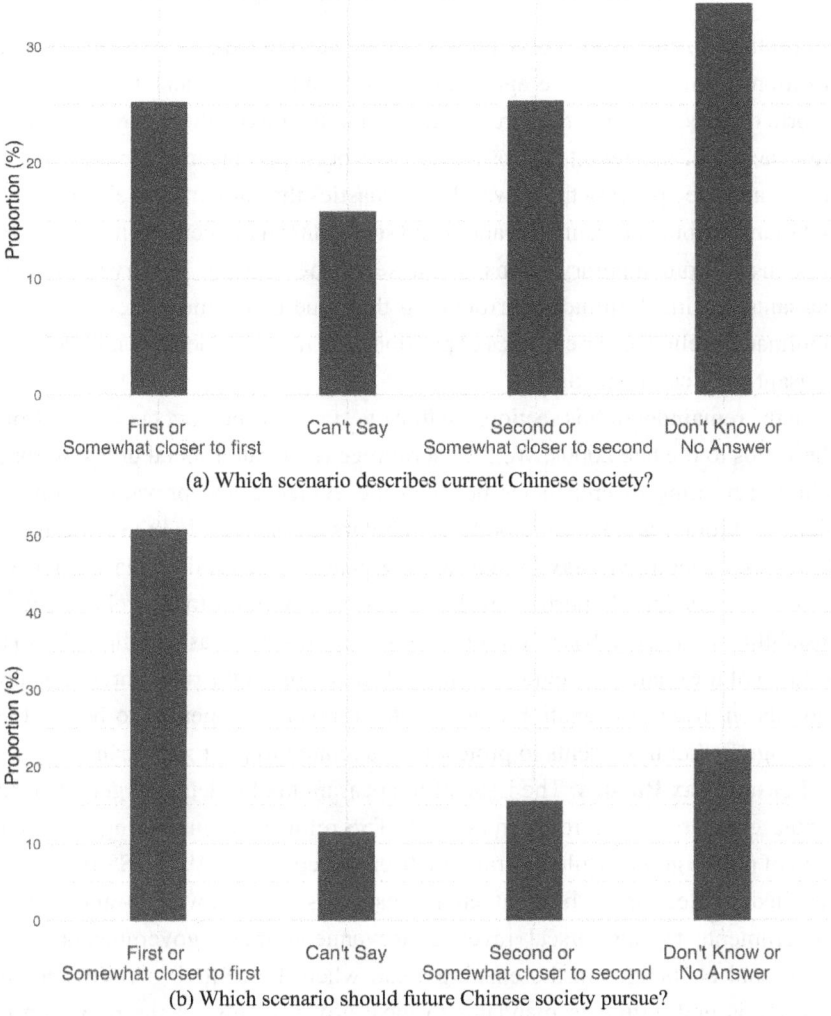

Figure 15 Current and prefer welfare state in China (The World Value Survey)

Note: This figure is based on Questions V145B and V145E in the 2010 WVS survey data.

a civic duty. Second, Chinese urbanites overwhelmingly prefer public goods and services over redistribution in return for taxation. The lack of political demand suggests that taxation may not be a salient issue – at least among urbanites – in their dealing with the government.

4.1.2 Taxation and the political behavior of rural residents

In contrast to urbanites, rural households have more direct experience with taxation, primarily because agricultural taxes and government fees represent a form of direct taxation they frequently encounter. Given the nature of agricultural taxation, tax revolts by peasants have been pivotal in fomenting social unrest and precipitating the downfall of dynasties throughout China's history.[58] Scholars attribute peasant grievances and social unrest to onerous and illegal tax burdens in contemporary China. Because of the scarcity of survey data on peasants' political attitudes surrounding the issue of taxation, they have predominantly relied on case studies of petitions and mass incidents as indicators of peasant political behavior.

In the remainder of this section, we first overview the peasant tax burden from the 1990s to the late 2000s. We then scrutinize tax-related social unrest in rural China, revealing discrepancies between the evidence and prevailing conclusions. Although an extensive body of scholarship emphasized the widespread heavy and illegitimate tax burden among peasants in rural China during the 1990s, a considerable portion of the evidence pertaining to tax-related social instability is notably based on anecdotal accounts and case studies. A close reading of the qualitative evidence suggests that most of the rural unrest may not have been driven by taxation alone; instead, taxation appeared to be used as leverage for rural residents to protest issues related to poor governance.

Peasant Tax Burden. The issue of the peasant tax burden emerged after the Chinese government introduced the 1994 TSS reform, decentralizing the provision of public goods while centralizing fiscal revenue. The 1994 TSS reform, as detailed in Section 3, brought enormous pressure to township and village governments to raise fiscal revenue. Revenue-strapped governments faced additional challenges in the ensuing years when the central government frequently issued unfunded mandates to local governments for the provision of public goods and services, thereby exacerbating the financial burden on peasants.

The tax burden borne by peasants emanates from various sources. Bernstein and Lü (2003) categorize these sources into five distinct types: (1) state taxes, (2) township and village fees, (3) compulsory labor, (4) miscellaneous fees, and (5) fines. These types manifest a form of direct taxation. Although state taxes like the agricultural tax (农业税) and its associated subtax (三提五统) amount to a relatively small share of the peasant tax burden, informal taxes stemming from fees and fines imposed by township and village governments are often

---

[58] See discussion in Bianco (2001) and Perry (1985). The fear of tax revolt left the Qing dynasty a long-lasting legacy of underinvestment in its fiscal capacity (Zhang 2022).

excessive and have become a major source of peasant–state conflict (Bernstein and Lü 2003; Thaxton 2016). Crucially, these taxes exhibit a regressive, not progressive, nature: The proportion of the tax burden relative to peasant income is higher among impoverished households and in less developed regions (Khan and Riskin 1998; Tao, Liu, and Zhang 2003).

Rising rural unrest in the early 1990s later captured the attention of the Chinese central government, which had initiated a series of policies in the early 2000s to reduce the peasant tax burden and expand social spending in education, healthcare, and pensions.[59] Consequently, the peasant financial burden has been radically reduced: The average burden declined from 10% of their agricultural income in the mid-1990s to less than 4% in 2004.[60] Although these policies mitigated the state tax burden on peasants, a noticeable surge occurred in ad hoc administrative fees and fundraising for public goods (Ma, Liu, and Tao 2010), indicating a substitution effect between formal and informal taxation.

In addition, the extent of tax reduction varies significantly across regions and among rural households. Deconstructing the tax burden by region and decile from 1988 to 2013 in the CHIP survey, Hoken and Sato (2020) show rural households in the bottom decile always have the highest effective tax rates, amounting to 14.82% and 14.22% in 1988 and 1995, respectively. Although the effective tax rates for this decile sharply declined to 0.27% in 2007 after the Chinese government's agricultural tax reform, it rose slightly to 1.49% in 2013. Meanwhile, rural households in Central China had the highest effective tax rate in 1988 (6.40%) and 1995 (6.81%), twice as much as those in Eastern and Western China. By 2013, the effective tax rate across these three regions became more homogenous, ranging from 0.22% in Eastern China to 0.28% in Western China.

Taxation as the Catalyst for Rural Unrest. Given the coincidence of the uptick in the peasant tax burden and rising rural unrest in China, scholars have unsurprisingly drawn the conclusion that the peasant tax burden was the primary culprit in rural instability in 1990s China. Among the first to link them, Bernstein and Lü (2003) trace the proliferation of their informal tax burden to the early 1990s, arguing that these burdens precipitated protests and violence in rural China. Citing evidence from a series of case studies based on news reporting in Hong Kong, these authors contend that peasants articulated their resentment toward the excessive tax burden through collective actions,

---

[59] For the agricultural tax reform, see Göbel (2010). For the expansion of social spending in rural China, see Huang (2014) and Lü (2014).
[60] See Figure 4.1 in Cai (2010: 73).

manifesting in protests and violent confrontations with local governments. Some of these events involved as many as 200,000 people or more.[61]

Subsequently, scholars of contentious politics have presented additional qualitative evidence to bolster this assertion (Cai 2010; O'Brien and Li 2006; Takeuchi 2014; Thaxton 2016); however, after the central government's fiscal reforms in the early 2000s – abolished agricultural tax and expanded rural social spending – tax-related unrest in rural China appeared to decline. Ong (2015) documented over 2,500 cases of social unrest between 2003 and 2012, but only 0.4% (9 out of 2,528) of the incidents were motivated by tax-related issues. Tong and Lei (2010) investigated large-scale mass incidents in China from 2003 to 2009, finding only 0.8% (2 out of 248 mass incidents) linked to taxes. In his interviews with peasants, Takeuchi (2014) observes that the reduction of the tax burden has minimized villagers' grievances toward local cadres due to taxation in the 2000s.

Taxation as the Primary Source of Revolt or as Leverage? A closer scrutiny of the evidence presented in this strand of scholarship reveals some puzzling discrepancies. The trend toward social unrest not only deviates from the trajectory of the peasant tax burden but, as suggested by the referenced case studies, also indicates that peasants employ taxes as leverage in their negotiations with the state to address issues extending beyond the realm of taxes.

To start, data presented in Cai (2010) suggest a contradiction in the trends of the tax burden and the amount of social unrest in China in the 1990s. For instance, the peasant tax burden peaked around 1994 and 1995, and it declined precipitately after 1996 (Cai 2010: 73). By contrast, the number of petitions to the central government radically increased after 1995 (Cai 2010: 23). Bianco (2001) makes a similar observation by comparing peasant grievance directed toward government policies and rural unrest since 1949. The grain procurement from late 1953 and the ensuing collectivization were the most unpopular policies in rural China, the land reform of the early 1950s and the household responsibility system of the 1980s, most popular. Regardless, peasant resistance from 1953 to 1978 was the lowest despite unpopular state rural policies.[62] Bianco concludes that the overall political environment plays a more important role in shaping political behaviors than the tax burden.

---

[61] See Table 5.1 in Bernstein and Lü (2003: 126–127) for the number of people involved in this social unrest across China. A caveat is warranted with the statistics presented in this table: The primary source is an anti-CCP tabloid (争鸣) in Hong Kong, which may have exaggerated the figures.

[62] Note that Perry (1985) has documented some sporadic violence against the state due to land reform and the collectivization campaign in the 1950s.

We suggest an alternative explanation for this contradiction between the tax burden and rural unrest: Peasants have used taxation as leverage in their contention with the state. Specifically, detailed case studies in earlier scholarship elucidate peasants' grievances, showing they did not exclusively revolve around taxation. Instead, the grievances extended to a wide range of issues, including village finance, land disputes, IOUs, the one-child policy, and village cadre corruption. A closer examination of existing case studies reveals that peasants refused to make their tax payments as a form of resistance against governance issues unrelated to taxation. Simply put, tax noncompliance is the "weapon of the weak" (Scott 1985). Instances of violence typically arose only after township and village officials failed to address their grievances through peaceful means and instead resorted to coercion in attempting to collect tax payments.

Hence, rising rural unrest may not necessarily be solely attributed to the tax burden; instead, villagers use their tax payments as leverage to demand resolutions of other issues. Indeed, scholars of contentious politics echo a similar observation, contending that peasants often employ tax evasion as a strategic tool against the state in response to a range of grievances (Cai 2010; Li and O'Brien 1996). A comprehensive analysis of contentious politics in rural China, drawn from the work of both Chinese and international scholars, suggests that the rise of social unrest can be attributed to factors including the growing rights consciousness among peasants, perceptions of relative deprivation, the emergence of informal institutions, rural cadre corruption, and the weakness of rural governance structures instead of the sole issue of taxation (Xiao 2005).

One empirical study sheds light on this alternative explanation, indicating that poor village governance, not the tax burden, is the primary source of rural unrest. Hou, Liu, and Lü (2024) discover a perplexing pattern wherein rural social unrest in the form of mass petitions and mass incidents has notably increased since the abolition of the agricultural tax in the early 2000s. Using evidence from panel data at the village level, these authors show that village cadres play a crucial role in mediating conflicts arising from the implementation of unpopular policies in rural China. An important implication of this study is that village cadres could serve as intermediaries to help the state manage social instability; therefore, peasant–cadre relations, not the tax burden alone, is the genuine catalyst for social unrest in rural China.

4.2 Taxation and the Political Behavior of Firms

Despite being the primary target of the state's fiscal extraction policy, Chinese firms have not engaged in active political endeavors to lobby for policy changes.

The absence of political activism among Chinese businesses could be attributed to the overall political environment in China, which prevents any organizations from collectively exerting their influence on government policymaking, especially at the highest level. Most taxes paid by firms manifest as indirect taxation, such as VAT and business taxes, allowing them to pass the tax burden to consumers; however, the absence of political activism among firms does not imply passivity in response to the state's fiscal extraction. Instead, Chinese businesses frequently employ various atomized strategies to lower their tax burden, either through illegal tax evasion or by seeking preferential tax subsidies.

In the remainder of Section 4.2, we first provide a succinct overview of the tax burden faced by Chinese firms, then delve into their political behavior in response to their tax obligations. We find that establishing political connections and seeking preferential treatment have been the primary strategies for Chinese businesses to mitigate their tax burden. Firms that cannot afford these strategies seek legal and illegal means to dodge their obligations.

4.2.1 Business Tax Burden

By 2013, the Chinese government formally stipulated seventeen types of business taxes, which can be categorized as taxes on goods and services, taxes on business profits, and taxes on international trade (Chen et al. 2021). Collectively, these have accounted for more than 90% of the tax revenue in China. Among these taxes, VAT, corporate income tax, and business tax held the top three positions in terms of the share of tax revenue. Notably, Chinese firms also make social security contributions akin to payroll taxes in the United States and social security taxes in Europe; they amount to an increasing share of tax payments from Chinese firms.

Tax Burden by Ownership Type. Chinese businesses comprise private, state-owned, and foreign-invested enterprises. An administrative tax survey conducted by the SAT of China from 2007 to 2011 shows that 80% of the enterprises in the tax survey data are private enterprises, and approximately 13% are foreign-invested enterprises (FIEs); less than 10% are SOEs.[63] Upon disaggregating the overall tax contributions based on ownership types, each category accounted for approximately one-third of the total tax payments. Chen et al. (2021) show that from 2007 to 2011, private enterprises contributed approximately 39.3%, while SOEs and FIEs contributed 36.8% and 23.9%, respectively.

---

[63] See Chen et al. (2021) for more details.

To assess the genuine tax burden facing businesses, scholars have focused on corporate income tax. One conventional measure of the business tax burden is the effective tax rate (ETR) – the average rate at which a firm's pretax profit is taxed. By this metric, Chinese businesses' ETRs have declined over time, with substantial variations based on ownership type. Analyzing public listed companies in China from 2004 to 2009, Luo and Yang (2013) find that median ETRs declined from 21.3% in 2004 to 17.8% in 2009. They divided the companies into three categories: Private enterprises, central SOEs, and local SOEs.[64] Their data indicate that private enterprises have slightly lower ETRs than SOEs; however, local SOEs have much higher ETRs than central SOEs. This finding aligns with Liu and Li (2012), who tracked public listed companies in China for a longer period (1998–2010). They find that the median ETR is 22.19% for local SOEs and 18.10% for central SOEs; private enterprises fall between them, with a median ETR of 18.86%. Cui (2015) surveys several studies on ETRs among Chinese firms, concluding that local SOEs always have the highest ETRs while central SOEs and private firms have lower ones. Furthermore, Cui suggests that higher ETRs faced by local SOEs are primarily influenced by the imperative revenue demand from local governments in China.

Tax Burden by Sector. Besides ownership type, Chinese firms in various sectors encounter different tax burdens because of state tax policies. For instance, the BT-to-VAT reform as well as the subsequent VAT reforms have not only changed the VAT tax rate but also introduced various preferential VAT exemptions and premium reductions for smaller firms as well as enterprises in manufacturing, wholesale, and retail.[65] In addition, Chinese businesses can reduce their corporate income tax through the loss carry-forward and tax credits targeting foreign joint ventures and high-tech industries as well as pollution prevention and control enterprises.[66] Chen et al. (2021), using data from 2008 to 2011, shows that industries like information technology, entertainment, finance, and insurance have the lowest effective corporate income taxes while real estate, construction, mining, transportation, and warehousing had the highest.

4.2.2 Firm Behavior

Despite their role as primary contributors to the Chinese government's tax revenue, Chinese businesses have rarely employed their taxation obligations to leverage

---

[64] Central SOEs are those controlled by various ministries at the central government level. Local SOEs are those controlled by provincial, prefectural, and sometimes county governments.

[65] China's Tax Incentives for the Manufacturing Sector in 2023 (www.china-briefing.com/news/china-preferential-tax-policies-for-manufacturing-sector/).

[66] See a summary by PWC (https://taxsummaries.pwc.com/peoples-republic-of-china/corporate/taxes-on-corporate-income?utm_source=chatgpt.com).

political engagement. One may attribute the inaction of Chinese businesses to the nature of the one-party state in China. Specifically, since 1949 the CCP has systematically inhibited any organizations that could potentially overcome the collective action problem and advance their political claims. Chinese businesses were subject to political repression and coercion during the radical political campaigns under Mao. Although economic reforms since 1978 have bolstered the economic power of elites and increased CCP favor, scholars have suggested that these "red capitalists" are allies, not opponents, of the state (Chen and Dickson 2010). Notably, the NPCSC delegated the power of taxation to the State Council in 1985; therefore, the State Council, MOF, and SAT dominate the legislating process of taxation, leaving very limited space for business lobbying through the legislature.

Given their substantial tax burden, for Chinese businesses – keen economic actors driven by profit maximization – to remain passive would be irrational. Indeed, while Chinese businesses may not be able to advance political claims akin to their counterparts in democracies, they actively pursue alternative strategies to alleviate their tax burden or seek economic benefits in return for taxation. The political environment in China is likely to compel Chinese businesses to employ strategies to benefit their individual firms, but they do not lobby policy changes that could benefit the entire sector; that is, businesses in China are unlikely to build a broad coalition to advance policy change.

Firm Strategies to Alleviate the Tax Burden. Like businesses in many other countries, Chinese firms attempt to alleviate their tax burden through legal and illegal means. On one hand, some Chinese businesses engage in illegal activities like tax noncompliance, tax evasion, or even bribery. Especially for small businesses lacking political clout, tax evasion resembles the "weapon of the weak" that rural households employ. On the other hand, some firm owners and managers are deeply embedded in the state elite network while others are indispensable contributors to central and local government revenue; therefore, these businesses could use tax payments as leverage to seek economic benefits from the state.

Studies on the effective tax rates faced by Chinese firms reveal significant variation across ownership types, reflecting their differing political leverage in reducing tax burdens. Specifically, central SOEs tend to have lower ETRs compared to local SOEs and private enterprises. Cui (2015) contends that SOEs constitute by far the most powerful and effective tax lobbies, resulting in lower ETRs. The formidable political influence wielded by central SOEs stems from the deep entrenchment of SOE managers within the elite network of the CCP at the highest echelons. By contrast, local SOEs and private enterprises have no such power, limiting their ability to obtain preferential treatment in tax policies, with the exception of those firms with high asset mobility.[67] Similar to firms in other countries, these firms attempt to establish political connections with government officials as a strategy to reduce their tax burden.[68] In one study, Luo and Yang (2013) find that a political connection could reduce ETRs for private firms and local SOEs but not for central SOEs.[69] This result is hardly surprising because central SOEs already have strong political connections with the state. Hou (2019) and Zhang (2021) provide qualitative evidence, illustrating that local entrepreneurs strategically use their positions in local legislative bodies to cultivate advantageous political connections. This strategic maneuver, in turn, assists their firms in mitigating tax pressures and burdens, such as reducing the likelihood of tax auditing (Lin et al. 2018).

Although establishing political connections is a desirable strategy, not all firms can pursue this strategy at will, especially many smaller SOEs and private firms. Facing limited political options, these firms explore loopholes in tax policies and even tax evasion as the last resort. Tsai (2007) offers some evidence of the pervasive tax evasion behavior by private entrepreneurs, suggesting that more than 80% of private businesses engaged in some form of tax evasion from 1994 to 1995. Cui (2022) argues that the Chinese tax administration favors a model emphasizing self-declaration and inspections by firms. This approach, however, creates ample opportunities for tax evasion. Tian and Zhao (2008) provide illuminating evidence of the strategic interaction and bargaining taking place between township tax bureaus and small firms through an ethnographic study in one county in China, showing that taxes on local businesses were negotiated between state tax collectors and business owners.

Firm Strategies for Preferential Treatment. In addition to a low tax burden, firms aspire to secure preferential treatments from the state. Because of the absence of formal channels (e.g., campaign finance and business lobbying) to engage in politics, Chinese businesses have sought to foster political connections with central – and most often – local officials to secure preferential treatment for their businesses (Kennedy 2005; Kung and Ma 2018).

Politics in China is highly personal. In contemporary China, firms have leveraged their political connections not only for tax relief but also to secure better

---

[67] See Zhang (2019) and Chen and Hollenbach (2022) on the role of political connection and tax burden reduction in China. Section 6 covers the implications of local governments' "race-to-the-bottom" tax competition.

[68] For comparative studies of political connections and firm tax burden, see Faccio (2006).

[69] This finding contrasts with Han, Li, and Oi (2022), who reveal that local SOEs with political connections pay a higher VAT. The discrepancies between these two studies can be attributed to different type of taxes that they evaluate: Han, Li, and Oi (2022) focus on VAT while Luo and Yang (2013) study ETRs based on corporate income tax.

access to bank credit and loans,[70] secure lower prices in land acquisitions,[71] alleviate regulatory pressure,[72] obtain government subsidies,[73] remove the entry barrier to capital markets,[74] and even receive legal protection.[75] This preferential treatment bolsters the financial standing of private firms, resulting in enhanced sales, profits, and, in some cases, improved stock market performance.[76]

Given the importance of political connections, Chinese businesses have adopted several strategies to secure a helping hand from the state. To this end, SOEs enjoy a comparative advantage over private businesses, thanks to their integration into the state nexus.[77] Private businesses traditionally rely on cultivating personal relationships with powerful politicians, and in recent years scholars have noted several novel strategies: to become delegates in national and local legislative and consultative bodies – the People's Congress and Chinese People's Political Consultative Conference (Hou 2019; Truex 2016); to establish political connections through the revolving-door exchange, engaging in the hiring and compensation of officials or their relatives via lucrative positions in their companies;[78] and to participate in the government initiated antipoverty campaign in order to mitigate the political scrutiny they face.[79]

Despite an upswing in political activism aimed at securing preferential policy treatment, only limited evidence suggests that businesses strategically leverage their tax obligations to achieve this objective. Although scholars have emphasized the crucial role of SOEs and private businesses in assisting local governments to achieve their revenue targets, the relatively small number of scholars who have delved into what firms gain in return from fiscal extraction by local governments is hardly surprising.[80] Lei (2021) conducted a rare study showing a reciprocal relationship between government and businesses involving the issue of taxation. He finds that businesses receiving preferential treatment (e.g., credit access or tax reduction) offer greater assistance through corporate income payments; furthermore, he provides suggestive evidence that firms receive greater subsidies because of their support of local government revenues.

---

[70] See Bai et al. (2020), Cong et al. (2019), Lei (2021), and Li et al. (2008).
[71] Chen and Kung (2019); Chen et al. (2022).
[72] Fisman and Wang (2015).
[73] Li (2024).
[74] Bao et al. (2016); Fan et al. (2007).
[75] Ang and Jia (2014).
[76] Bai et al. (2020); Li (2008); Truex (2014).
[77] See Cui (2022); Han, Li, and Oi (2022).
[78] Chen et al. (2022); Kung and Ma (2018); (Li 2024).
[79] Lin, Shengqiao (2025).
[80] Cui (2015); Han, Li, and Oi (2022).

4.3 Conclusion

To what extent does taxation motivate political activism among individuals and firms in China? The short answer is this: To a very limited degree. This section reviews existing scholarship on the behavior of both citizens and businesses, providing scant evidence that taxation serves as a highly contentious issue shaping state–society relations in China. One may even argue the tax-related social unrest in rural China during the early 1990s was an exception, because it was driven by ad hoc government fees imposed on peasants. In this strand of literature, a direct link between the tax burden and social unrest remains elusive once we delve deeply into the existing evidence.

However, the design of tax policies has a profound impact on citizens' tax perceptions and political attitudes (Campbell 2018). Scholars have attributed the absence of political activism centering on taxation to the structure of the Chinese government's fiscal capacity: The reliance on indirect taxation. PIT has never exceeded 10% of government revenue, with its share and tax base shrinking after recent reforms raised the exemption threshold. Meanwhile, the Chinese government abolished agricultural taxes in 2006, effectively restricting its capacity for fiscal extraction through direct taxation in rural China. For Chinese businesses, corporate income tax is the only form of direct taxation, amounting to less than 20% of the total tax payment to the government. The rest of the tax payment consists of indirect taxes, such as VAT and business tax, whose burden businesses can shift to consumers. Together, the minimal share of direct taxation on the incomes of individuals and businesses implies that it hardly motivates any political action, especially those requiring clearing the hurdle of collective action.

Although this argument has its merits, various perplexing developments indicate that it might be incomplete. First, the Chinese government reversed its course to mitigate the rising share of PIT in the mid-2010s through several tax reforms that seemed largely to favor affluent economic elites despite having been designed to benefit ordinary citizens. As demonstrated in Kao, Lü, and Queralt (2024), Chinese economic elites prefer greater political rights over the provision of public goods in return for taxation, which offers one explanation for the Chinese government's policy change. This is also consistent with Martin's (2023) finding that some African states strategically underinvest in fiscal capacity to alleviate citizens' political demands.

Second, among Chinese firms the lack of political activism aimed at taxation remains enigmatic. The key question is how economic elites choose to pursue responses to taxation between collective action and atomized strategy. Why do some firms focus on political connections while others seek preferential treatment outside taxation? Do major tax contributors leverage their payments for state benefits? Remaining underexplored in the literature, these questions warrant further investigation.

5 Unintended Consequences of Taxation in China

The absence of political activism stemming from taxation in contemporary China is not necessarily a blessing for the government: Limited tax bargaining could undermine its responsiveness and accountability, as in many African countries (Prichard 2015). Although the government may rely on indirect taxation and limit taxation on personal income and wealth to ease potential tension, doing so may inadvertently produce unintended consequences, ultimately straining state–society relations. Moreover, the centralization of revenue and decentralization of public spending since the 1994 TSS reform, coupled with the government's desire to spur economic growth through public investment, have prompted local governments to raise fiscal revenues through nontax sources. In Section 5, we explore two types of unintended consequences: (1) constraints on any potential tax reforms to expand direct taxation on individual income and wealth and (2) adverse effects of nontax revenue stemming from rising local government debt, land-driven fiscal extraction, and forbearance in government degradation.

5.1 Curse of Limiting Direct Taxation

PIT had steadily trended upward from the 1990s to the 2000s, propelled by China's rapid economic growth; but the trend was disrupted in the late 2000s by successive tax cuts aimed at boosting consumption and public support.[81] Not only have these tax reductions led to an underinvestment of bureaucratic capacity for taxing personal income and wealth, but they also inadvertently intensified citizens' sensitivity to any future expansion of individual taxation.

5.1.1 Underinvestment in Extractive Capacity of Taxing Individuals

Taxing personal income is a challenging task for any state. To effectively collect PIT, the government must develop a robust information capacity for monitoring individual income streams and a formidable deterrence capacity for detecting and punishing instances of tax evasion, and China is no exception. Economic liberalization reforms in China since 1978 have significantly diminished the proportion of employment in SOEs and the public sector. Simultaneously, rapid technological changes have generated ample economic opportunities in the informal since the 1990s. Moreover, the rise of the capital

---

[81] See Section 3 for the motivation behind PIT reform.

market in China allows many Chinese citizens, particularly affluent ones, to draw their income from nonsalary sources like private investment and the financial and housing markets. Consequently, the Chinese government faces a daunting challenge to comprehensively assess individual income in today's diverse market economy.

Moreover, China's tax bureaucracy has prioritized investment in collecting indirect and business taxes over personal income and wealth taxation. The Chinese government has initiated four major waves of investment to enhance the state taxation infrastructure since 1994 under the Golden Tax Project (金税工程). These investments committed substantial financial and human resources to upgrading the state's information system and compliance technology for tax collection.[82] Most of the investments center on facilitating the collection of VAT, business tax, and corporate income tax, but not personal taxes. The only exception is the 2018 launch of a smartphone app to assist Chinese citizens in filing their annual PIT, yet the SAT invested little to build a national information system to track individual income and wealth from diverse sources, especially from nonsalary sources. To date, the tax bureau mostly relies on self-reporting by affluent taxpayers.

The lack of strong taxation capacity for PIT results in widespread tax evasion. Using microlevel data or simulation, scholars have estimated that the evasion rate, mostly from nonsalary sources, spans 30% to 80% across years and regions.[83] At times, government tax agencies initiate audits on high-profile individual taxpayers like film stars, sports figures, and social media influencers; however, the auditing of these individuals does not typically originate from tax bureaus but instead from scandals and corruption charges initially attracting public attention.

The absence of property taxation in urban China is another clear indicator of the government's unwillingness to tax individuals for fear of potential political repercussions. Rapid urbanization and economic growth have led to a booming real estate market in urban China since 1999. By 2022, private homeownership became a major source of household wealth in urban China, accounting for 63.9% of household wealth,[84] a figure that dwarfs the 28.5% observed in the

---

[82] Notably, the CCP Central Committee announced the need to strengthen administrative capacity for direct taxation as a priority for future tax reforms at its Third Plenary Session of the 20th Central Committee on July 18, 2024 ("中共中央关于进一步全面深化改革、推进中国式现代化的决定 [Decision of the CPC Central Committee on Further Comprehensively Deepening Reform and Promoting Modernization with Chinese Characteristics]"), www.gov.cn/zhengce/202407/content_6963770.htm (accessed September 9, 2024).

[83] See summary in Yan, Xia, and Chen (2016).

[84] See "2022 Trends in China Household Wealth" (https://chfs.swufe.edu.cn/info/1031/1736.htm), produced by the Survey and Research Center for China Household Finance, Southwest University of Finance and Economics.

United States. Nonetheless, Chinese homeowners are not subject to the annual property tax levied in developed economies.

The failure to expand property tax stems from a lack of political will, not administrative constraints. Specifically, the state has embarked on a series of initiatives designed to lay the groundwork for property tax collection, such as the 2011 pilot programs in Shanghai and Chongqing targeting affluent individuals, followed by an effort to establish a national homeownership registration database in 2015. When President Xi Jinping, arguably the most dominant Chinese leader since Deng Xiaoping, attempted to expand the property tax in fifteen major cities in 2021, he failed to roll out this reform.[85]

One key reason for China's reluctance in taxing personal income and wealth surrounds the formidable (political and economic) costs and limited benefits associated with the expansion of personal tax. Specifically, seeking compliance in paying tax on personal income and wealth requires considerable bureaucratic capacity, but the return on the investment remains minimal – at least for the near future. After all, PIT has constituted less than 10% of state tax revenue since the 1980s. The shrinking base of PIT after 2018 further disincentivized central and local tax bureaus to allocate critical human and capital resources to collect PIT. Importantly, the government is deeply concerned that intensifying PIT collection could hinder domestic consumption, especially with the Chinese economy facing significant headwinds in recent years. Finally, the Chinese government has championed tax reduction as a propaganda tool to bolster popular support; reversing this trend could generate significant political backlash. In fact, the next section demonstrates that PIT is associated with highly sensitive public discourse in Chinese society.

5.1.2 Sensitivity to Individual Taxation among the Public

Paradoxically, the Chinese government's endeavors to alleviate the individual tax burden have inadvertently heightened the salience of the issue. Through persistent advocacy for tax cuts under the guise of enhancing the welfare of citizens, the government fosters an unrealistic expectation among the public that PIT will always remain low. Consequently, the government would face significant resistance if leaders were to expand direct taxation, even to alleviate income inequality.

---

[85] Xi made a bold attempt at introducing property tax collection in major cities as part of his Common Prosperity agenda in autumn 2021; however, this plan met resistance within the party and was subsequently canceled because of the difficult macroeconomic conditions exacerbated by the COVID-19 pandemic. See "In Tackling China's Real-Estate Bubble, Xi Jinping Faces Resistance to Property-Tax Plan," *Wall Street Journal* (October 19, 2021).

Table 3 2018 PIT reform

	Before 2018	**After 2018**
Exemption threshold	¥ 3,500 per month per person, tax exemption calculated monthly	¥ 5,000 per month per person, tax exemption calculated annually
Deductions	No	Expenditure on children's education, taxpayers' own continuing education, medical treatment for serious illness, housing loan interest or rent, and support for elders
Collection methods	Withheld by employer, information not integrated	Withheld by employer, SAT automatically collects most income information and calculates tax liability for taxpayers
Self-report	Optional self-report for individuals whose annual income is higher than ¥ 120,000	Self-report for tax deductions and tax return
Tax salience	Low	High

Specifically, the 2018 PIT reform introduced several features enhancing the visibility of PIT even though its burden remains low for most individuals. For example, the SAT launched a website and mobile app to streamline taxpayer compliance.[86] Both unintentionally draw attention to PIT because most taxpayers had previously paid only through paycheck deductions. Furthermore, the introduction of itemized deductions, intended to alleviate tax burdens, also encourages taxpayers to compare their liabilities before and after applying these deductions. Table 3 summarizes changes in the 2018 PIT reform.

Figure 16a illustrates the frequency of news articles covering PIT in over 500 Chinese newspapers, including party, industry, and general-purpose newspapers at all levels, published since 2000. We observe exceedingly active media coverage from 2006 to 2011, corresponding to three major PIT reforms elevating the

---

[86] Chen, Jia, "Tax deduction app goes online," *China Daily*, February 1, 2019, www.chinadaily.com.cn/a/201901/02/WS5c2c04ffa310d91214051f69.html (last accessed October. 6, 2022).

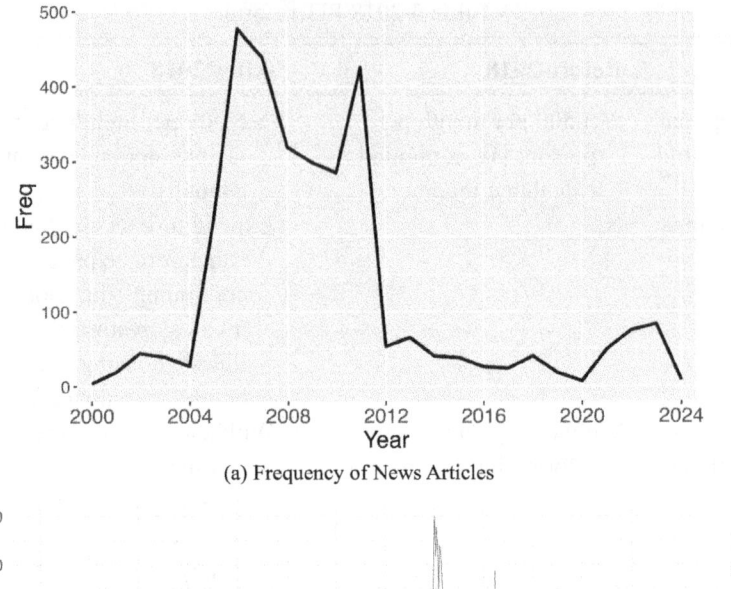

(a) Frequency of News Articles

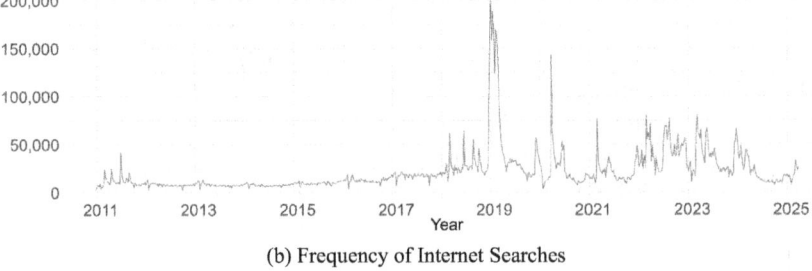

(b) Frequency of Internet Searches

Figure 16 Frequency of news articles and internet searches on personal income tax (2000–2023).

Source: Data for (a) derived from China Core Newspapers Full-Text Database (CCND). Data for (b) were obtained from the Baidu Index based on the following search keywords in Chinese for individual income tax and income tax exemption thresholds (个人所得税, 个税, 个税起征点).

exemption threshold for PIT in 2006, 2008, and 2011. Furthermore, the 2018 tax reform and the subsequent introduction of the personal deduction in 2019 and 2023 generated another small uptick in media coverage.

In contrast, internet search patterns related to PIT unveil a distinct trend during the same period. Figure 16b illustrates the frequency of internet search terms related to PIT on Baidu.com, a major search engine in China. As depicted, the 2011 tax reform spurred minimal internet searches on PIT during that year despite the active media coverage illustrated in Figure 16a. The 2018 PIT reform, however, garnered significant public attention. During the NPC discussions in March 2018, the reform drew intense scrutiny from citizens and was hailed as a successful example of "open-door legislation."[87] Importantly, Figure 16b shows that urban residents actively seek online information related to PIT every year now, particularly during the period from March 1 to June 30, when Chinese urbanites file their taxes to secure returns through itemized deductions.

Chinese residents' sensitivity to PIT was on full display when the NPC solicited public comments on drafts and revisions of laws and regulations. Periodically, the NPC releases the draft of some proposed laws and revisions on its website, soliciting public comments for thirty days. From 2010 to 2023, the NPC released fifteen drafts of laws on various taxes for public comment. Figure 17 shows engagement in the 2011 and 2018 PIT revisions was the highest among these fifteen tax laws, far surpassing the 2010 Transportation Tax Law and the 2023 VAT Law (2nd Revision), which ranked third and fourth, respectively.

In comparison, we turn to public discourse on VAT, where the tax burden is indirectly borne by citizens. Indeed, we find muted public interest in VAT. First, Figure 18a plots the frequency of news articles on VAT in the media, showing that they reached their peak in the late 2000s, a few years before the Chinese government initiated a pilot program converting the business tax to a VAT for a few industries in Shanghai in 2012. The Chinese government's full implementation of BT-to-VAT reform in 2016 across all industries for the entire country received moderate media coverage. Only when the state expanded deductions and reduced the tax rate after 2020 did the media revive coverage of VAT.

Meanwhile, Chinese citizens showed lukewarm interest in VAT even when the peak number of news articles covering it was greater than that for PIT. Figure 18b reveals that internet searches for VAT and related topics were the most frequently searched in 2016 when the state rolled out the reform converting business tax to VAT for the entire country. Crucially, both the duration and peak number of daily searches for VAT were smaller than those for PIT, and the public comments for NPC bills on VAT in 2022 and 2023 also attracted less attention.

Property tax is another example of major direct taxation receiving significant attention from urbanites. For instance, the Shanghai and Chongqing governments each pioneered pilot programs for annual property tax in 2011, generating fervent media coverage resembling that for policy changes in PIT (Figure 19a). Over the next decade media coverage of property tax reform

---

[87] According to the Baidu "Twin Conferences" Index, the PIT exemption threshold had the highest peak search value of 62,390 during the annual NPC and CPPCC conferences, followed by institutional reform at 38,183 (https://baijiahao.baidu.com/s?id=1596278915770810849&wfr=spider&for=pc, accessed on September 22, 2024).

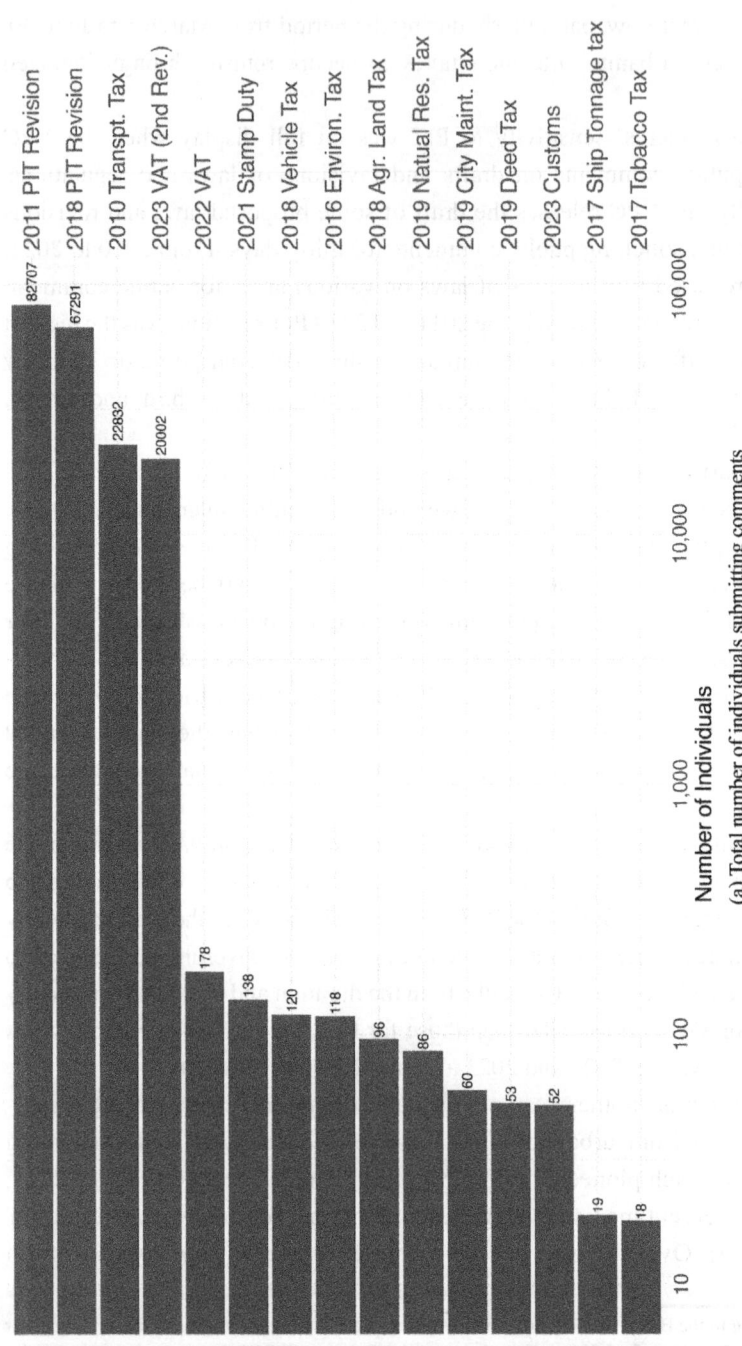

Figure 17 Public comments on tax-related laws at the NPC (2010–2023).

Note: Authors' dataset obtained from NPC website (www.npc.gov.cn/flcaw/).

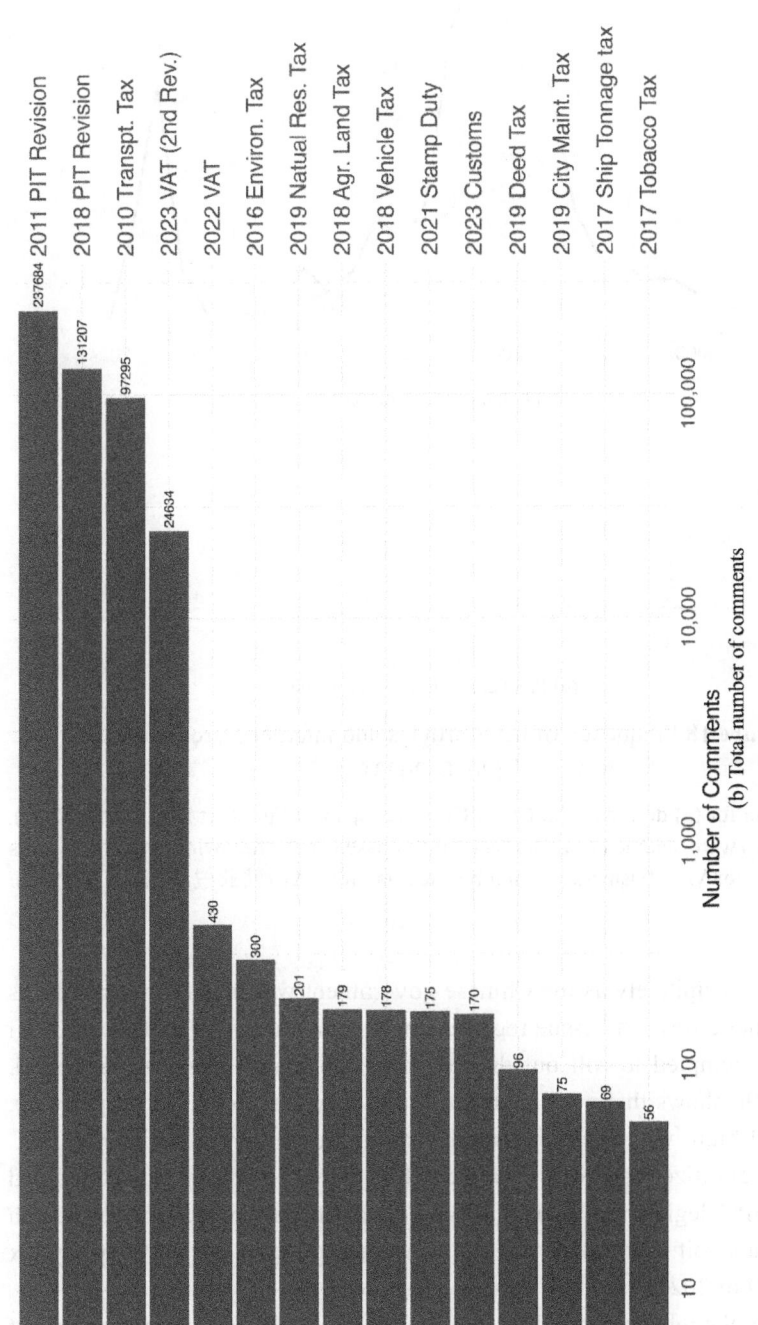

Figure 17 (cont.)

(b) Total number of comments

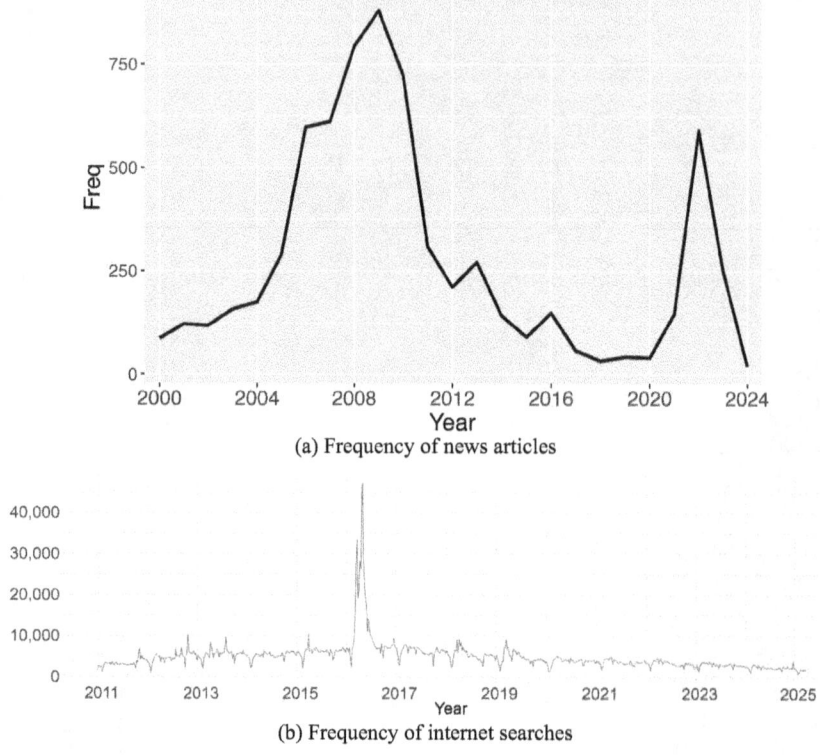

Figure 18 Frequency of news articles and internet searches on VAT (2010–2023).

Note: Data for (a) derived from China Core Newspapers Full-Text Database (CCND). Data for (b) were obtained from the Baidu Index based on the following search keywords in Chinese for VAT, business tax, and business tax for VAT (营业税, 增值税, 营改增).

declined precipitately as the Chinese government was unable to expand this tax to other cities. This issue regained media attention in late 2021, when Xi Jinping attempted to roll out the tax to fifteen major cities. Nevertheless, Figure 19b shows that public interest in the potential rollout of property tax remained high, with internet searches spiking each spring during the NPC sessions, as citizens anxiously waited to find out whether it would be included in the NPC legislation agenda for the year. In particular, internet search sparked a significant uptick when Xi was attempting to roll out property tax in the fall of 2021.

In sum, the reliance on indirect taxation by the Chinese government has set a false expectation of a continuous low PIT rate for individual taxpayers. In addition, the introduction of tax deductions perpetually revives public interest in

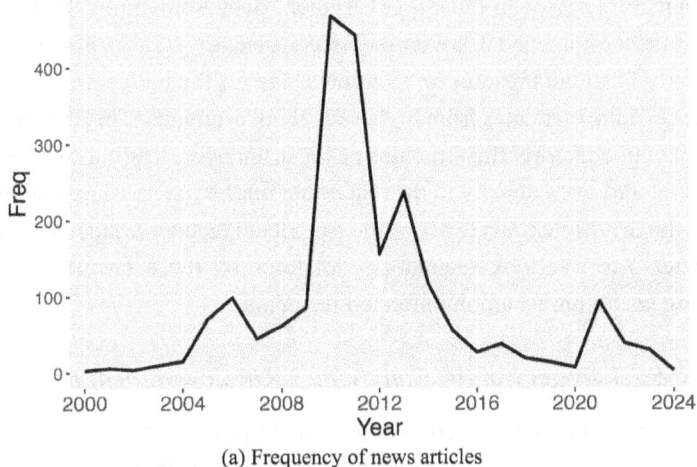

(a) Frequency of news articles

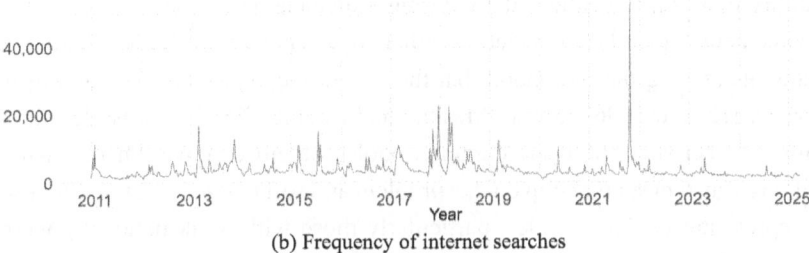

(b) Frequency of internet searches

Figure 19 Frequency of news articles and internet searches on property tax (2010–2023).

Note: Data for (a) derived from China Core Newspapers Full-Text Database (CCND). Data for (b) were obtained from the Baidu Index based on the following search keywords in Chinese for property taxes (房产税, 房地产税).

PIT. These deductions incentivize urban taxpayers to actively pursue tax refunds from the state and calculate their effective tax rates. Contrary to the intentions of policymakers, the salience of direct taxation has steadily increased among Chinese citizens.

5.2 Unintended Consequences of Relying on Nontax Revenue

Section 3 demonstrates that local governments face increasing pressure to adopt strategies to raise fiscal revenues to meet expenditure demands while maintaining political stability. This unintentionally sparks new issues threatening the stability of the fiscal system and undermining governance. Specifically, local governments, eager to stimulate economic growth through public investment, are constrained by insufficient fiscal revenue; therefore, they resort to opportunistic behavior in raising government debt, sometimes through illegal means. Furthermore, local governments consistently turn to nontax revenue, particularly local land resources, to compensate for the budgetary shortfall and increase revenue mandates from higher-level governments. This dependence on nontax revenue distorts the structure of local finances, leading to government corruption, and overcapacity in the real estate market, increasing land disputes. Finally, the drive to extract tax revenue from local businesses incentivizes local governments to overlook regulatory violations by these businesses, thereby triggering social unrest among affected residents.

5.2.1 Tragedy of the Commons: Local Government Debt

Local governments are acutely aware that despite the central government's stated commitment to refrain from bailouts, its prioritizing macroeconomic stability makes intervention likely during a financial crisis. This type of fiscal arrangement typically engenders a soft budget constraints for local governments, increasing the likelihood that they spend beyond their revenue-raising capacity (Kornai 1986; Kornai, Maskin, and Roland, 2003); that is, decentralization exacerbates the basic common-pool problem of government finance. Although current scholarship on this problem and soft budget constraint focuses on representative democracies, particularly those with weak national governments and fiscal transfer-dependent local governments, we find that these insights are also highly relevant to China despite its strong central government.

Soft budgetary constraint became an acute issue faced by local governments in the last two decades, especially when the Chinese central government implemented the 4 trillion CNY stimulation program to bolster economic growth, responding to the global financial crisis in 2008. Although the central government prefers fiscal discipline and macroeconomic stability, this policy goal has been sacrificed for the other policy goals of stimulating economic growth (保增长) and maintaining employment (保就业) to prevent social unrest. The fiscal expansion program allowed Chinese local governments to employ local financing vehicles to borrow and spend on their own behalf (Bai, Hsieh, and Song 2016). Furthermore, China's unique combination of highly centralized political power and highly decentralized economic authority, which Xu (2011) called "regionally decentralized authoritarianism," exacerbated the tragedy of the commons: Local governments engage in intense competition for economic growth because outperforming their peers enhances their prospects in the promotion tournament. Under China's investment-driven growth model, borrowing became a preferred strategy for local governments. Access to local state banks (for backdoor financing) through local government finance vehicles (融资平台) serves as financial leverage for land

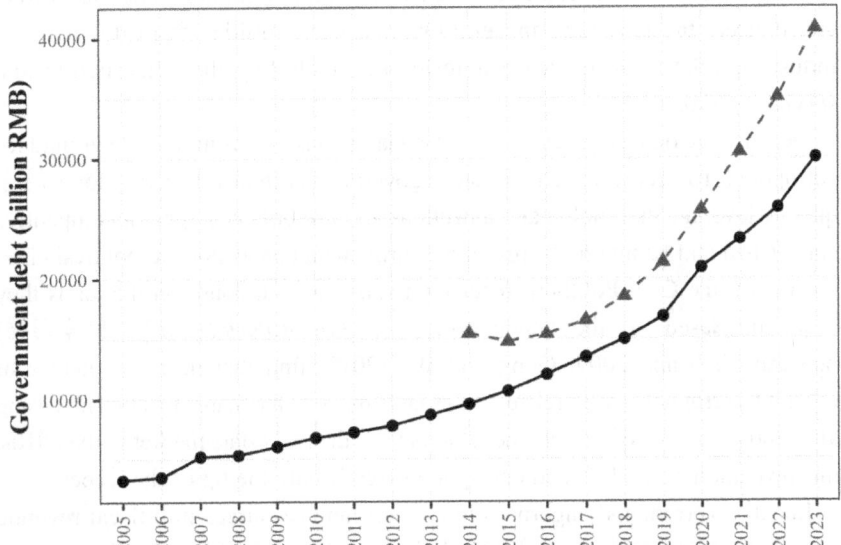

Figure 20 Rising central and local government debts (2015–2023).

Note: Data obtained from the MOF. The central government debt was about 3,000 billion Yuan in 2005, 15,000 billion in 2018, and 30,000 billion in 2023. The local governments' debt was 15,000 billion in 2014 and reached 40,000 billion in 2023.

transfer revenues, empowering local governments with the capacity of unchecked borrowing (Liu et al. 2022; Zhou 2012). Overall, the Chinese government, especially local governments, has accumulated alarming debts, which could potentially threaten the stability of the financial system (Figure 20).

5.2.2 Perils of Land-Driven Local Fiscal Extraction

The amendment to the Land Administration Law of China (中华人民共和国土地管理法) in 1998 offered a much-needed lifeline to the revenue-strapped local governments since the 1994 TSS reform.[88] The amendment enabled local governments to raise nontax revenues through the repurposing of public lands for industrial and real estate purposes. Subsequently, revenue from land sales and leases has evolved into an increasingly vital source of local governments' budget, surging from less than 10% of

---

[88] For full content of the law, see www.npc.gov.cn/npc/c30834/201909/d1e6c1a1eec345e ba23796c6e8473347.shtml (accessed September 1, 2020).

government revenue in 2000 to 63.4% in 2013 (Han and Kung 2015). Importantly, the land-resource-based development model generates direct and indirect tax revenues and employment opportunities from downstream industries related to the real estate market, including the construction and services sectors.

Dependence on land revenue has turned land transactions into fertile ground for corruption. To secure land from local governments, real estate developers frequently leverage their political connections and use bribery to gain a competitive edge. Chen and Kung (2019) reveal that firms with connections to political elites serving on the CCP Politburo received a substantial discount on the lands they acquired. Based on the announcement in *Procuratorial Daily* (检察日报) between 2000 and 2009, Gong and Wu (2012) find that nearly a quarter of reported corruption cases relate to the land market, its share of total increasing after 2005. Given the booming development of the real estate market in the 2010s, this revelation of land-related corruption cases is only the tip of the iceberg.

Local governments' eagerness to convert land resources into fiscal revenue reveals that they often prioritize their own interests, along with those of businesses, at the expense of citizen welfare. For instance, the Land Administration Law of China permits the government to acquire rural land for "public purposes"; however, the interpretation of public purposes is intentionally ambiguous and expansive: Any conversion of land use in the pursuit of industrial, infrastructural, and commercial development could potentially be construed as serving public purposes. The law constrains peasant compensation to thirty times the average annual agricultural productivity or less. Consequently, the law typically does not align with the interests of peasants because land compensation is determined by its past agricultural output value rather than its considerably higher market value once the transaction concludes (Pils 2005).

Scholars have documented land disputes as one of the primary sources of social unrest in contemporary China.[89] To expropriate land from peasants, local governments have employed various tactics – ranging from relational pressure, soft and hard coercion, and violence outsourced to nonstate actors like local clan members and even the mafia[90] – to accomplish their objectives. Unsurprisingly, peasants and urbanites respond to these government tactics via formal and informal channels; for instance, peasants have submitted letters of petition to government agencies of various levels to voice grievances. In addition, they also stage mass protests in

---

[89] See Ong and Göbel (2014), Heurlin (2016), and Whiting (2011).
[90] See Hurst et al. (2014) and Ong (2022).

response to the predatory behavior of local governments and real estate developers. In some instances, peasants have engaged in violence against government officials.

Beyond land-related issues, a cozy state–business relationship frequently contributes to lax government regulations, subsequently resulting in myriad governance issues. Dependent on local businesses for tax revenues and employment, Chinese local governments overlook violations of regulations concerning labor standards, workplace safety, and environmental protection. The forbearance of regulation enforcement, in turn, results in numerous labor disputes (Hurst 2009; Lee 2007; Rho 2023) and environmental degradation (Ong and Göbel 2014; Kahn and Zheng 2016), undermining state–society relations.

5.3 Conclusion

In this section, we examine several unintended consequences of the Chinese government's taxation strategy, which relies on indirect taxation and nontax revenues to mitigate the visibility of tax burdens. First, the Chinese government's repeated emphasis on reducing tax burdens for individuals has unintentionally heightened Chinese citizens' sensitivity to direct taxation. This sensitivity is further exacerbated during economic downturns, constraining the government's ability to explore new revenue sources to meet fiscal demands. Second, local governments, under pressure to meet tax targets and drive economic growth set by higher-level authorities, engage in risky behavior that leads to rising government debt and worsening state–society relations. These actions – not only jeopardizing the stability of China's financial system but also undermining state legitimacy, a priority for the central government – reflect its fiscal trilemma well. Lack of tax bargaining weakens governance quality, and China is no exception.

6 Final Reflections

Is studying political behaviors stemming from taxation in China misguided, considering tax policies are driven by state preferences, not the actions of citizens and firms? At first glance, major tax policy changes in China appear to stem from strategic interaction among central and local governments. The central government initiated various tax reforms to address the unintended consequences of earlier fiscal policies subsequently undermined by the local governments as they used their discretionary power to distort the implementation of tax policies. Even according to earlier scholarship on social unrest in rural China, tax grievances alone have rarely been sufficient for peasants to overcome the collective action problem and participate in costly revolts against local officials. Instead, they were incited by various rural governance issues, taxation serving merely as the straw that broke the camel's back.

Although economic growth, expansion of fiscal capacity, and political stability can mutually reinforce one another – embodying the "pillars of prosperity" proposed by Besley and Persson (2011) – the emergence of this development cluster remains elusive for the Chinese central government, which continues to navigate the trilemma among revenue extraction, economic growth, and political stability. Specifically, the central government faces several tradeoffs in its strategies.

First, reliance on indirect taxation could effectively reduce citizens' tax consciousness, but such a strategy results in regressive taxation and high levels of inequality. Paradoxically, recent tax reduction on individuals inadvertently heightened their sensitivity to direct taxation, potentially undermining further direct tax reforms. Second, the revenue-sharing arrangement favors the central government over local governments, forcing the latter to rely on nontax revenues, such as land revenue and administrative fees, which undermine the development of state fiscal capacity. Third, the CCP's dual strategies of repression and cooptation to maintain stability have become increasingly costly. Rising expenditure for stability maintenance, coupled with an aging population and growing citizen expectations, puts pressure on the government to mandate high social contributions, equivalent to PIT. This, in turn, risks social unrest and contradicts tax reduction policies aimed at spurring economic growth.

Although the state may mitigate the immediate impact of taxation, it remains vulnerable to its indirect and downstream consequences. To this end, the peculiar role of taxation in China's current state–society relations raises several important issues associated with firm and citizen behaviors not yet fully explored. To begin, we should not assume that Chinese firms are "toothless" in their response to state revenue demands. From the perspective of the Chinese government, revenue mobilization remains the foundation of its strategy for fiscal extraction. This approach has successfully bolstered the state's fiscal capacity but at the expense of the rule of law in the realm of taxation. Although this strategy has provided stability in government finances and reduced uncertainty in state planning, local governments frequently engage in negotiations with firms and employ tactics to encourage tax payments aligned with the government's revenue targets rather than based on actual business revenues and transactions. Consequently, the strategic interaction among local governments and firms could generate profound implications for local governance.

Relatedly, how Chinese firms navigate and respond to taxation remains an understudied area. Given their crucial role in contributing to the state's tax and nontax revenues, the discretionary power of local governments offers businesses a vital opportunity to leverage their tax contributions for economic and even political benefits. Although Chinese business elites have not actively engaged in seeking political representation in a fashion similar to those documented in early modern European states or postcommunist countries, they have pursued atomized strategies like seeking preferential tax treatment or policy benefits. Examining when and how firms leverage taxation to pursue strategies offers valuable insights into the dynamics of state–business relations.

For instance, many Chinese firms have exhibited behavior akin to "migration economy" (候鸟经济) by taking advantage of local governments' desire to promote economic growth and expand the local tax base. Specifically, these firms strategically establish their operations in jurisdictions that offer preferential tax treatment and other policy benefits from local governments. When these advantages expire, they relocate to other areas to secure renewed benefits – unless the current local government extends or provides new incentives. In essence, these firms leverage their asset mobility to create bidding wars among local governments. Will these behaviors lead to a "race-to-the-bottom" tax competition that undermines China's fiscal capacity? Furthermore, does asset mobility allow firms to seek only economic benefits, or do they try to obtain some political influence in local politics?

With regard to individual taxpayers, if the Chinese government expands direct taxation, would this strategy heighten taxation as a contentious issue in state–society relations? The Chinese government is unlikely to deviate from the revenue mobilization model because the state disdains economic fluctuation from market forces. Instead, it prefers to be in the driver's seat in managing economic activities and revenue collection. The reliance on indirect taxation and nontax revenue has so far deflected the potential tension stemming from taxation, but China's ailing economy and demographic shift are likely to shrink the tax base and undermine existing strategies for revenue mobilization, potentially pressuring the government to pursue direct taxation. Particularly in the time of economic crisis, the government will confront the same austerity dilemma – cut public spending or raise taxes – faced by many European states[91] (Alesina, Favero, and Giavazzi 2019). What are the key parameters shaping the government strategies to address the austerity dilemma?

These questions are of both theoretical and policy significance. If history serves as a guide, the CCP faced a similar situation in 1941, when it encountered a fiscal shock following the KMT's withdrawal of financial aid, which had accounted for nearly 90% of the CCP's government revenues at the time. In a detailed study, Lü (2025) shows how the CCP employed the tactic of "mobilized compliance" in grain levies, a form of direct taxation imposed on rural

---

[91] This reflects the limitation of development clusters.

households. By deploying grassroots party organizations to mobilize peasants, the CCP strategically shifted tensions arising from grain levies upon rural households themselves and incentivized peasants to truthfully reveal their grain production and comply with CCP grain levies. Subsequently, the tactic of "mobilized compliance" has been employed in urban taxation after 1949 (Chen 2005). Whether the CCP can replicate its success in mobilizing direct taxation without the backdrop of interstate wars and expand this strategy beyond the rural context remains an open question.

References

Academic Affairs Division of the CCP Central Party School. 2015. 十一届三中全会以来党和国家重要文献选编 [*Selected Important Documents of the Party and the State since the Third Plenary Session of the 11th Central Committee*]. Beijing: CCP Central Party School Press.

Acemoglu, Daron. 2005. "Politics and Economics in Weak and Strong States." *Journal of Monetary Economics*, Swiss National Bank Special Issue, 52:1199–1226.

Alesina, Alberto, Carlo Favero, and Francesco Giavazzi. 2019. "Effects of Austerity: Expenditure- and Tax-Based Approaches." *Journal of Economic Perspectives* 33 (2):141–162.

Alm, James, and Benno Torgler. 2006. "Culture Differences and Tax Morale in the United States and in Europe." *Journal of Economic Psychology* 27:224–246.

Andersen, Jørgen J., and Michael L. Ross. 2014. "The Big Oil Change: A Closer Look at the Haber–Menaldo Analysis." *Comparative Political Studies* 47 (7):993–1021.

Ang, Yuen Yuen, and Nan Jia. 2014. Perverse Complementarity: Political Connections and the Use of Courts among Private Firms in China. *The Journal of Politics* 76 (2):318–332.

Bai, Chong-En, Chang-Tai Hsieh, and Zheng Michael Song. 2016. "The Long Shadow of a Fiscal Expansion." National Bureau of Economic Research. NBER Working Paper No. 22801. www.nber.org/system/files/working_papers/w22801/w22801.pdf.

Bai, Chong-en, Chang-Tai Hsieh, and Zheng Song. 2020. "Special Deals with Chinese Characteristics." *NBER Macroeconomics Annual* 34:341–379.

Bao, Xiaolu, Sofia Johan, and Kenji Kutsuna. 2016. "Do Political Connections Matter in Accessing Capital Markets? Evidence from China." *Emerging Markets Review* 29:24–41.

Basinger, Scott, and Mark Hallerberg. 2004. "Remodeling the Competition for Capital: How Domestic Politics Erases the Race to the Bottom." *American Political Science Review* 98 (2):261–276.

Bates, Robert H., and Da-Hsiang Donald Lien. 1985. "A Note on Taxation, Development, and Representative Government." *Politics & Society* 14 (1):53–70.

Beramendi, Pablo, and David Rueda. 2007. "Social Democracy Constrained: Indirect Taxation in Industrialized Democracies." *British Journal of Political Science* 37 (4):619–641.

Bernstein, Thomas P., and Xiaobo Lü. 2003. *Taxation without Representation in Contemporary Rural China*. New York: Cambridge University Press.

Besley, Timothy, Ethan Ilzetzki, and Torsten Persson. 2013. "Weak States and Steady States: The Dynamics of Fiscal Capacity." *American Economic Journal: Macroeconomics* 5 (4):205–235.

Besley, Timothy, and Torsten Persson. 2009. "The Origins of State Capacity: Property Rights, Taxation, and Politics." *The American Economic Review* 99:1218–1244.

Besley, Timothy, and Torsten Persson. 2011. *Pillars of Prosperity: The Political Economics of Development Clusters*. Princeton, NJ: Princeton University Press.

Bianco, Lucien. 2001. *Peasants without the Party: Grass-Roots Movements in Twentieth-Century China*. Armonk, NY: M.E. Sharpe.

Bonney, Richard. 1999. *The Rise of the Fiscal State in Europe, C. 1200–1815*. New York: Oxford University Press.

Botev, Jarmila, Jean-Marc Fournier, and Annabelle Mourougane. 2016. A Reassessment of Fiscal Space in OECD Countries. Paris. *OECD Economics Department Working Papers*, No. 1352, OECD Publishing, Paris, https://doi.org/10.1787/fec60e1b-en.

Bräutigam, Deborah, Odd-Helge Fjeldstad, and Mick Moore. 2008. *Taxation and State-Building in Developing Countries: Capacity and Consent*. New York: Cambridge University Press.

Brewer, John. 1989. *The Sinews of Power: War, Money, and the English State, 1688–1783*. 1st Am. ed. New York: Alfred A. Knopf.

Cai, Yongshun. 2010. *Collective Resistance in China: Why Popular Protests Succeed or Fail*. Stanford, CA: Stanford University Press.

Campbell, Andrea. 2018. "Tax Designs and Tax Attitudes." *The Forum* 16 (3):369–98.

Centeno, Miguel Angel. 2002. *Blood and Debt: War and the Nation-State in Latin America*. University Park: Pennsylvania State University Press.

Central Committee of CCP. 2024. "Decision of the Central Committee of the Communist Party of China on Further Comprehensively Deepening Reform and Promoting Chinese-Style Modernization."

Cheibub, José Antonio. 1998. "Political Regimes and the Extractive Capacity of Governments: Taxation in Democracies and Dictatorships." *World Politics* 50 (3):349–376.

Chen, Jie, and Bruce J. Dickson. 2010. *Allies of the State: China's Private Entrepreneurs and Democratic Change*. Cambridge, MA: Harvard University Press.

Chen, Ling, and Hao Zhang. 2021. "Strategic Authoritarianism: The Political Cycles and Selectivity of China's Tax-Break Policy." *American Journal of Political Science* 65 (4):845–861.

Chen, Ting and James Kung, 2019. "Busting the 'Princelings': The Campaign against Corruption in China's Primary Land Market." *The Quarterly Journal of Economics* 134 (1):185–226.

Chen, Ting, Li Han, James Kung, and Jiaxin Xie, 2023. "Trading Favours through the Revolving Door: Evidence from China's Primary Land Market." *The Economic Journal* 133 (649):70–97.

Chen, Yongfa. 2005. "中共建國初期的工商稅收：以天津和上海為中心 [Chinese Taxation of the Urban Private Sector in the Early 1950s: An Examination of Tianjin and Shanghai]." 中央研究院近代史研究所集刊 *[The Journal of Modern History Institute]* 48:137–187.

Chen, Zhao, Xian Jiang, Zhikuo Liu, Juan Carlos Suárez Serrato, and Daniel Yi Xu. 2022. "Tax Policy and Lumpy Investment Behaviour: Evidence from China's VAT Reform." *The Review of Economic Studies* 90 (2):634–674.

Cong, Will, Haoyu Gao, Jacopo Ponticelli, and Xiaoguang Yang. 2019. "Credit Allocation under Economic Stimulus: Evidence from China." *Review of Financial Studies* 32 (9):3412–3460.

Congdon, William, Jerey R. Kling, and Sendhil Mullainathan. 2009. "Behavioral Economics and Tax Policy." *National Tax Journal* 6 (3):375–386.

Cui, Wei. 2012. "税收立法高度集权模式的起源 [The Origin of China's Highly Centralized Tax Legislation]." 中外法学 *[Peking University Law Journal]* 24 (4):762–781.

———. 2014. "China's Business-Tax-to-VAT Reform: An Interim Assessment." *British Tax Review* 5:617–641.

———. 2015. "Administrative Decentralization and Tax Compliance: A Transactional Cost Perspective." *University of Toronto Law Journal* 65 (3):186–238.

———. 2022. *The Administrative Foundations of the Chinese Fiscal State*. Cambridge: Cambridge University Press.

D'Arcy, Michelle, and Marina Nistotskaya. 2017. "State First, then Democracy: Using Cadastral Records to Explain Governmental Performance in Public Goods Provision." *Governance* 30 (2):193–209.

Deng, Xiaoping. 1983. 邓小平文选第二卷 *[Selected Works of Deng Xiaoping (Vol. 2)]*. Beijing: People's Publishing House.

———. 1993. 邓小平文选第三卷 *[Selected Works of Deng Xiaoping (Vol. 3)]*. Beijing: People's Publishing House.

Dickson, Bruce J. 2016. *The Dictator's Dilemma: The Chinese Communist Party's Strategy for Survival*. Oxford: Oxford University Press.

Dincecco, Mark. 2009. "Fiscal Centralization, Limited Government, and Public Revenues in Europe, 1650–1913." *The Journal of Economic History* 69 (1):48–103.

2011. *Political Transformations and Public Finances: Europe, 1650–1913*. Cambridge: Cambridge University Press.

Dixit, Avinash, Gene M. Grossman, and Elhanan Helpman. 1997. "Common Agency and Coordination: General Theory and Application to Government Policy Making." *Journal of Political Economy* 105 (4):752–769.

Duara, Prasenjit. 1988. *Culture, Power, and the State: Rural North China, 1900–1942*. Stanford, CA: Stanford University Press.

Easterly, William, and Sergio Rebelo. 1993. "Fiscal Policy and Economic Growth." *Journal of Monetary Economics* 32 (3):417–458.

Edin, Maria. 2003. "Remaking the Communist Party-State: The Cadre Responsibility System at the Local Level in China." *China: An International Journal* 1 (1):1–15.

Editorial Board of Contemporary China's Finance. 1990. 中国社会主义财政史参考资料, *1949–1985 [References to the History of Chinese Socialist Finance (1949–1985)]*. Beijing: Zhongguo caizheng jingji chubanshe.

Esping-Andersen, Gøsta. 1990. *The Three Worlds of Welfare Capitalism*. Princeton, NJ: Princeton University Press.

Faccio, Mara. 2006. "Politically Connected Firms." *American Economic Review* 96 (1):369–386.

Fairfield, Tasha. 2015. *Private Wealth and Public Revenue in Latin America: Business Power and Tax Politics*. Cambridge: Cambridge University Press.

Fan, Joseph, T. J. Wong, and Tianyu Zhang. 2007. "Politically Connected CEOs, Corporate Governance, and Post-IPO Performance of China's Newly Partially Privatized Firms." *Journal of Financial Economics* 84 (2):330–357.

Fang, Hanming, and Jin Feng. 2020. "The Chinese Pension System." In *The Handbook of China's Financial System*, ed. Marlene Amstad, Guofeng Sun, and Wei Xiong. Princeton, NJ: Princeton University Press, 421–446.

Fariss, Christopher J., Therese Anders, Jonathan N. Markowitz, and Miriam Barnum. 2022. "New Estimates of over 500 Years of Historic GDP and Population Data." *Journal of Conflict Resolution* 66 (3):553–591.

Finkelstein, Amy. 2009. "E-ZTax: Tax Salience and Tax Rates." *The Quarterly Journal of Economics* 124 (3):969–1010.

Fisman, Raymond, and Yongxiang Wang. 2015. "The Mortality Cost of Political Connections." *The Review of Economic Studies* 82 (4): 1346–1382.

Flores-Macías, Gustavo A. 2018. "Building Support for Taxation in Developing Countries: Experimental Evidence from Mexico." *World Development* 105:13–24.

Fochmann, Martin, Dirk Kiesewetter, Kay Blaufus, Jochen Hundsdoerfer, and Joachim Weimann. 2010. "Tax Perception – An Empirical Survey." Arqus Discussion Paper No. 99. http://dx.doi.org/10.2139/ssrn.1707443.

Frazier, Mark W. 2010. *Socialist Insecurity: Pensions and the Politics of Uneven Development in China*. Ithaca, NY: Cornell University Press.

Gao, Peiyong. 2013. "营改增" 的功能定位与前行脉络 [Business Tax to VAT Reform's Function and Prospectus]." 税务研究 *[Taxation Research]* 7:3–10.

Garcia, Maria Melody, and Christian Von Haldenwang. 2016. "Do Democracies Tax More? Political Regime Type and Taxation." *Journal of International Development* 28 (4):485–506.

Göbel, Christian. 2010. *The Politics of Rural Reform in China: State Policy and Village Predicament in the Early 2000s*. London: Routledge.

Goldscheid, Rudolf. 1917. *Staatssozialismus oder Staatskapitalismus: Ein Finanzsoziologischer Beitrag zur Lösung des Staatsschulden-Problems*. 2. und 3. verb. aufl. ed. Wien-Leipzig: Brüder Suschitzky.

Gong, Ting, and Alfred M. Wu. 2012. Central Mandates in Flux: An Empirical Study of Local Noncompliance in China. *Publius: The Journal of Federalism* 42 (2):313–333.

Haber, Stephen, and Victor Menaldo. 2011. "Do Natural Resources Fuel Authoritarianism? A Reappraisal of the Resource Curse." *American Political Science Review* 105 (1):1–26.

Han, Chaohua, Xiaojun Li, and Jean C. Oi. 2022. "Firms as Revenue Safety Nets: Political Connections and Returns to the Chinese State." *The China Quarterly* 251:683–704.

Han, Li, and James Kung. 2015. "Fiscal Incentives and Policy Choices of Local Governments: Evidence from China." *Journal of Development Economics* 116:89–104.

Hays, Jude C. 2011. "Globalization and Capital Taxation in Consensus and Majoritarian Democracies." *World Politics* 56 (1):79–113.

He, Wenkai. 2013. *The Paths toward the Modern Fiscal State: Early Modern England, Meiji Japan, and Qing China*. Cambridge, MA: Harvard University Press.

Herb, Michael. 2005. "No Representation without Taxation? Rents, Development, and Democracy." *Comparative Politics*:297–316.

Herbst, Jeffrey Ira. 2000. *States and Power in Africa: Comparative Lessons in Authority and Control*. Princeton, NJ: Princeton University Press.

Heurlin, Christopher. 2016. *Responsive Authoritarianism in China: Land, Protests, and Policy Making*. Cambridge: Cambridge University Press.

Hoken, Hisatoshi, and Hiroshi Sato. 2020. "Public Policy and Long-Term Trends in Inequality in Rural China." In *Changing Trends in China's*

Inequality: Evidence, Analysis, and Prospects, ed. Terry Sicular, Shi Li, Ximing Yue, and Hiroshi Sat. New York: Oxford University Press, 169–200.

Hou, Linke, Mingxing Liu, and Xiaobo Lü. 2024. "Disgruntled Cadres: How Tax Reduction Undermines Rural Governance." *Governance* 37 (3):751–769.

Hou, Yue. 2019. *The Private Sector in Public Office: Selective Property Rights in China*. New York: Cambridge University Press.

Huang, Xian. 2014. "Expansion of Chinese Social Health Insurance: Who Gets What, When and How?" *Journal of Contemporary China* 23 (89):1–29.

2020. *Social Protection under Authoritarianism: Health Politics and Policy in China*. New York: Oxford University Press.

Forthcoming. "China's Social Protection System and Reform." In *The Oxford Handbook of Social Protection in the Global South*, ed. Anis Ben Brik. Oxford: Oxford University Press.

Huang, Yasheng. 1996. *Inflation and Investment Controls in China: The Political Economy of Central-Local Relations during the Reform Era*. New York: Cambridge University Press.

2008. *Capitalism with Chinese Characteristics: Entrepreneurship and the State*. New York: Cambridge University Press.

Huntington, Samuel. 1968. *Political Order in Changing Societies*. New Haven, CT: Yale University Press.

Hurst, William. 2009. *The Chinese Worker after Socialism*. New York: Cambridge University Press.

Hurst, William, Mingxing Liu, Yongdong Liu, and Ran Tao. 2014. "Reassessing Collective Petitioning in Rural China: Civic Engagement, Extra-State Violence, and Regional Variation." *Comparative Politics* 46 (4): 459–482.

Jia, Ruixue, Masayuki Kudamatsu, and David Seim. 2015. "Political Selection in China: The Complementary Roles of Connections and Performance." *Journal of the European Economic Association* 13 (4):631–668.

Jin, Chongji, and Qun Chen. 2005. 陈云传 [*Biography of Chen Yun*]. Beijing: Central Literature Publishing House.

Jin, Hehui, Yingyi Qian, and Barry R. Weingast. 2005. "Regional Decentralization and Fiscal Incentives: Federalism, Chinese Style." *Journal of Public Economics* 89 (9–10):1719–1742.

Kahn, Matthew, and Siqi Zheng. 2016. *Blue Skies over Beijing: Economic Growth and the Environment in China*. Princeton, NJ: Princeton University Press.

Kao, Jay C., Xiaobo Lü, and Didac Queralt. 2024. "Do Gains in Political Representation Sweeten Tax Reform in China? It Depends on Who You Ask." *Political Science Research and Methods* 12 (1):146–165.

Kennedy, Scott. 2005. *The Business of Lobbying in China*. Cambridge, MA: Harvard University Press.

Khan, Azizur R., and Carl Riskin. 1998. Income and Inequality in China: Composition, Distribution and Growth of Household Income, 1988 to 1995. *The China Quarterly* 154:221–253.

Knight, John. 2013. "Inequality in China: An Overview." *The World Bank Research Observer* 29 (1):1–19.

Kornai, Janos, Eric Maskin, and Gerald Roland. 2003. "Understanding the Soft Budget Constraint." *Journal of Economic Literature* 41 (4):1095–1136.

Kornai, János. 1986. "The Soft Budget Constraint." *Kyklos* 39 (1):3–30.

Kung, James, and Chicheng Ma. 2018. "Friends with Benefits: How Political Connections Help to Sustain Private Enterprise Growth in China." *Economica* 85 (337):41–74.

Kuziemko, Ilyana, Michael I. Norton, Emmanuel Saez, and Stefanie Stantcheva. 2015. "How Elastic Are Preferences for Redistribution? Evidence from Randomized Survey Experiments." *American Economic Review* 105 (4):1478–1508.

Lan, Xiaohuan. 2021. 置身事内: 中国政府与经济发展 [*Insider's Role: Chinese Government and Economic Development*]. Shanghai: Shanghai ren min chu ban she.

Landry, Pierre F. 2008. *Decentralized Authoritarianism in China: The Communist Party's Control of Local Elites in the Post-Mao Era*. New York: Cambridge University Press.

Landry, Pierre F., Xiaobo Lü, and Haiyan Duan. 2018. "Does Performance Matter? Evaluating Political Selection Along the Chinese Administrative Ladder." *Comparative Political Studies* 51 (8):1074–1105.

Lardy, Nicholas R. 2014. *Markets over Mao: The Rise of Private Business in China*. Washington, DC: Peterson Institute for International Economics.

2019. *The State Strikes Back: The End of Economic Reform in China?* Washington, DC: Peterson Institute for International Economics.

Lee, Ching Kwan. 2007. *Against the Law: Labor Protests in China's Rustbelt and Sunbelt*. Berkeley: University of California Press.

Lee, Ching Kwan, and Yonghong Zhang. 2013. "The Power of Instability: Unraveling the Microfoundations of Bargained Authoritarianism in China." *American Journal of Sociology* 118 (6):1475–1508.

Lei, Yu-Hsiang. 2021. "Quid pro quo? Government-Firm Relationships in China." *Journal of Public Economics* 199:104427.

Levi, Margaret. 1988. *Of Rule and Revenue*. Berkeley: University of California Press.

2006. "Why We Need a New Theory of Government." *Perspectives on Politics* 4 (1):5–19.

Li, Lianjiang. 2016. Reassessing Trust in the Central Government: Evidence from Five National Surveys. *China Quarterly* 225: 100–121.

Li, Lianjiang, and Kevin O'Brien, 1996. Villagers and Popular Resistance in Contemporary China, *Modern China* 22 (1): 28–61.

Li, Ding, Xiaobo Lü, Shuang Ma, and Wenhui Yang. 2025. "The Shadow of Social Desirability Bias: Evidence from Reassessing the Sources of Political Trust in China." University of Texas Working Paper.

Li, Hongbin, and Li-An Zhou. 2005. "Political Turnover and Economic Performance: The Incentive Role of Personnel Control in China." *Journal of Public Economics* 89 (9–10):1743–1762.

Li, Xue, and Changdong Zhang. 2025. "Grassroots State Reconfiguration under Tax State Transition in Rural China." The China Review, 25 (3): 29–55.

Li, Zeren. 2024. Subsidies for Sale: Postgovernment Career Concerns, Revolving-Door Channels, and Public Resource Misallocation in China. *The Journal of Politics* 86(2): 704–719.

Lieberman, Evan S. 2003. *Race and Regionalism in the Politics of Taxation in Brazil and South Africa*. New York: Cambridge University Press.

Lieberthal, Kenneth. 1992. "Fragmented Authority." In *Bureaucracy, Politics, and Decision Making in Post-Mao China*, ed. Kenneth Lieberthal, and David Lampton. Berkeley: University of California Press, 1–32.

2004. *Governing China: From Revolution through Reform*. 2nd ed. New York: W. W. Norton.

Lieberthal, Kenneth, and Michel Oksenberg. 1988. *Policy Making in China: Leaders, Structures, and Processes*. Princeton, NJ: Princeton University Press.

Lin, Kenny Z., Lillian F. Mills, Fang Zhang, and Yongbo Li. 2018. "Do Political Connections Weaken Tax Enforcement Effectiveness?" *Contemporary Accounting Research* 35 (4):1941–1972.

Lin, Shengqiao. (2025) Addressing Risk by Doing Good: Business Response to Government Policy Initiative. *The Journal of Politics*.

Lin, Shuanglin. 2022. *China's Public Finance: Reforms, Challenges, and Options*. New York: Cambridge University Press.

Liu, Adam Y., Jean C. Oi, and Yi Zhang. 2022. "China's Local Government Debt: The Grand Bargain." *The China Journal* 87:40–71.

Liu, Jianwen. 2019. "个税改革的法治成果与优化路径 [The Rule of Law Achievements and Optimization Path of Personal Income Tax Reform]." 现代法学 *[Modern Law Science]* (2):22–34.

Liu, Kegu, and Kang Jia. 2008. 中国财税改革三十年 – 亲历与回顾 *[Thirty Years of China's Fiscal Reform: Personal Experience and Retrospect]*. Beijing: Jingji Kexue Chubanshe.

Liu, Shangxi, and Zhihua Fu. 2018.中国改革开放的财政逻辑 *(1978—2018) [The Fiscal Logic of China's Reform and Opening-Up (1978–2018)]*. Beijing: People's Publishing House.

Liu, Xing, and Xiaorong Li. 2012. "金字塔结构, 税收负担与企业价值: 基于地方国有企业的证据 [Pyramid Structure, Tax Burden, and Firm Valuation: Evidence from Local SOEs]." 管理世界 *[The Management World]* (8):91–105.

Liu, Yongzheng, Jorge Martinez-Vazquez, and Alfred M. Wu. 2017. "Fiscal Decentralization, Equalization, and Intra-provincial Inequality in China." *International Tax and Public Finance* 24 (2):248–281.

Liu, Zuo. 2021. 中国税制 *[Tax System of the People's Republic of China]*. 11 ed. Beijing: China Tax Press.

Lou, Jiwei. 2013. 中国政府间财政关系再思考 *[Rethinking China's Intergovernmental Fiscal Relationships]*. Beijing: China Fiscal and Economic Press.

Luo, Danglun, and Yuping Yang. 2013. 产权、政治关系与企业税负—来自中国上市公司的经验证据 [Property Rights, Political Connection, and Enterprise Tax Burden – Empirical Evidence Base on Chinese Listed Company]. 世界经济文汇 *[World Economic Papers]* 4:1–19.

Luttmer, Erzo, and Monica Singhal. 2014. "Tax Morale." *Journal of Economic Perspectives* 28 (4):149–168.

Lü, Bingyang. 2022. 央地关系: 寓活力于秩序 *[Central Local Relationship: Order with Dynamics]*. Beijing: Commercial Press.

Lü, Xiaobo. 2014. "Social Policy and Regime Legitimacy: The Effects of Education Reform in China." *American Political Science Review* 108 (2):423–437.

2015. "Intergovernmental Transfers and Local Education Provision – Evaluating China's 8–7 National Plan for Poverty Reduction." *China Economic Review* 33:200–211.

2025. *Domination and Mobilization: The Rise and Fall of Political Parties in China's Republican Era*. Cambridge: Cambridge University Press.

Lü, Xiaobo, and Pierre F. Landry. 2014. "Show Me the Money: Interjurisdiction Political Competition and Fiscal Extraction in China." *American Political Science Review* 108 (3):706–722.

Ma, Caichen, and Zaozao Zhao. 2019. 新中国预算建设70年 *[Seventy Years of Government Budgeting in China]*. Beijing: China Finance and Economic Press.

Ma, Yan, Mingxin Liu, and Ran Tao. 2010. "农户的税费和教育费负担的地区差异及其变动趋势 [The Evolution and Regional Variation of Tax Burden and Education Fees of Rural Hourseholds]." In 北京大学中国教育财政科学研究所政策咨询报告文集 *[Policy Reports by Chinese Institute of Education Finance Research at Peking University]*, ed. Rong Wang. Beijing: Jiao yu ke xue chu ban she, 1–13.

Manion, Melanie. 1985. "The Cadre Management System, Post-Mao: The Appointment, Promotion, Transfer and Removal of Party and State Leaders." *The China Quarterly* 102:203–233.

2023. *Political Selection in China: Rethinking Foundations and Findings*. New York: Cambridge University Press.

Mao, Zedong. 1991. 毛泽东文选 *[Selected Works of Mao Zedong]*. Beijing: People's Publishing House.

Martin, Cathie J. 1991. *Shifting the Burden: The Struggle over Growth and Corporate Taxation*. Chicago, IL: University of Chicago Press.

Martin, Lucy. 2023. *Strategic Taxation: Fiscal Capacity and Accountability in African States*: Oxford University Press.

Meltzer, Allan H., and Scott F. Richard. 1981. "A Rational Theory of the Size of Government." *Journal of Political Economy* 89 (5):914–927.

Montinola, Gabriella, Yingyi Qian, and Barry R. Weingast. 1995. "Federalism, Chinese Style: The Political Basis for Economic Success in China." *World Politics* 48 (1):50–81.

Moore, Mick. 2008. "Between Coercion and Contract: Competing Narratives on Taxation and Governance." In *Taxation and State-Building in Developing Countries: Capacity and Consent*, ed. Deborah Bräutigam, Odd-Helge Fjeldstad, and Mick Moore. New York: Cambridge University Press, 34–63.

Moore, Mick, Wilson Prichard, and Odd-Helge Fjeldstad. 2018. *Taxing Africa: Coercion, Reform and Development*. London: World Peace Foundation.

Morrison, Kevin. 2015. *Nontaxation and Representation: The Fiscal Foundations of Political Stability*. New York: Cambridge University Press.

Mulligan, Casey B., Ricard Gil, and Xavier Sala-i-Martin. 2004. "Do Democracies Have Different Public Policies than Nondemocracies?" *Journal of Economic Perspectives* 18 (1):51–74.

North, Douglass C., and Barry R. Weingast. 1989. "Constitutions and Commitment: The Evolution of Institutional Governing Public Choice in Seventeenth-Century England." *The Journal of Economic History* 49 (4):803–832.

O'Brien, Kevin. 1990. *Reform without Liberalization: China's National People's Congress and the Politics of Institutional Change*. New York: Cambridge University Press.

References

O'Brien, Kevin J., and Lianjiang Li. 1999. "Selective Policy Implementation in Rural China." *Comparative Politics* 31 (2):167–186.

O'Brien, Kevin, and Lianjiang Li. 2006. *Rightful Resistance in Rural China*. New York: Cambridge University Press.

OECD. 2019. *Tax Morale: What Drives People and Businesses to Pay Tax?* Paris: OECD.

Oi, Jean C. 1992. "Fiscal Reform and the Economic Foundations of Local State Corporatism in China." *World Politics* 45 (1):99–126.

Oi, Jean C., Kim Singer Babiarz, Linxiu Zhang, Renfu Luo, and Scott Rozelle. 2012. "Shifting Fiscal Control to Limit Cadre Power in China's Townships and Villages." *The China Quarterly* 211:649–675.

Ong, Lynette H. 2012. *Prosper or Perish: Credit and Fiscal Systems in Rural China*. Ithaca, NY: Cornell University Press.

2015. "Reports of Social Unrest: Basic Characteristics, Trends and Patterns, 2003–12." In *Handbook of Research on Politics in China*, ed. David SG. Goodman. Cheltenham: Edward Elgar, 345–359.

2022. *Outsourcing Repression: Everyday State Power in Contemporary China*. New York, NY: Oxford University Press.

Ong, Lynette H., and Christian Goebel. 2014. "Social Unrest in China." *China and the EU in Context. Insights for Business and Investors*.

Pan, Jennifer. 2020. *Welfare for Autocrats: How Social Assistance in China Cares for its Rulers*. New York, NY: Oxford University Press.

Pearson, Margaret, Meg Rithmire, and Kellee Tsai. 2023. *The State and Capitalism in China*. Cambridge ; New York, NY: Cambridge University Press.

Perry, Elizabeth. 1985. "Rural Violence in Socialist China." *The China Quarterly* 103:414–440.

Piketty, Thomas, and Nancy Qian. 2009. "Income Inequality and Progressive Income Taxation in China and India, 1986–2015." *American Economic Journal: Applied Economics* 1 (2):53–63.

Pils, Eva. 2005. "Land Disputes, Rights Assertion, and Social Unrest in China: A Case from Sichuan." *Columbia Journal of Asian Law* 19:235.

Prasad, Monica. 2012. *The Land of Too Much: American Abundance and the Paradox of Poverty*. Cambridge, MA: Harvard University Press.

2018. *Starving the Beast: Ronald Reagan and the Tax Cut Revolution*. New York: Russell Sage Foundation.

Prichard, Wilson. 2015. *Taxation, Responsiveness, and Accountability in Sub-Saharan Africa: The Dynamics of Tax Bargaining*. New York: Cambridge University Press.

Prichard, Wilson, Paola Salardi, and Paul Segal. 2014 "Taxation, Non-tax Revenue and Democracy: New Evidence Using New Cross-Country Data." *World Development* 109 (3):295–312.

Przeworski, Adam. 1990. *The State and the Economy under Capitalism*. New York: Harwood Academic.

Qian, Yingyi, and Barry R. Weingast. 1997. "Federalism as a Commitment to Reserving Market Incentives." *Journal of Economic Perspectives* 11 (4):83–92.

Qian, Yingyi, and Chenggang Xu. 1998. "Innovation and Bureaucracy under Soft and Hard Budget Constraints." *The Review of Economic Studies* 65 (1):151–164.

Qian, Yingyi, and Gerard Roland. 1998. "Federalism and the Soft Budget Constraint." *The American Economic Review* 88:1143–1162.

Queralt, Dídac. 2022. *Pawned States: State Building in the Era of International Finance*. Princeton, NJ: Princeton University Press.

Rho, Sungmin. 2023. *Atomized Incorporation: Chinese Workers and the Aftermath of China's Rise*. New York: Cambridge University Press.

Rong, Jingben. 1998. 从压力型体制向民主合作体制的转变: 县乡两级政治体制改革 *[From the Pressure-Based System to Democratic Cooperative System: Political Reform at the County and Township Level]*. Beijing: Zhongyang Bianyi Press.

Ross, Michael L. 2004. "Does Taxation Lead to Representation?" *British Journal of Political Science* 34 (2):229–249.

Ross, Michael. 2012. *The Oil Curse: How Petroleum Wealth Shapes the Development of Nations*. Princeton, NJ: Princeton University Press.

Rothstein, Bo. 2011. *The Quality of Government: Corruption, Social Trust, and Inequality in International Perspective*. Chicago: University of Chicago Press.

Sausgruber, Rupert, and Jean-Robert Tyran. 2005. "Testing the Mill Hypothesis of Fiscal Illusion." *Public Choice* 122 (1–2):39–68.

Scheve, Kenneth, and David Stasavage. 2016. *Taxing the Rich: A History of Fiscal Fairness in the United States and Europe*: Princeton University Press.

Schumpeter, Joseph. 1991. "The Crisis of the Tax State." In *The Economics and Sociology of Capitalism*, ed. Richard Swedberg. Princeton, NJ: Princeton University Press, 99–140.

Scott, James. 1985. *Weapons of the Weak: Everyday Forms of Peasant Resistance*. New Haven, CT: Yale University Press.

Shirk, Susan. 1993. *The Political Logic of Economic Reform in China*. Berkeley: University of California Press.

Slater, Dan. 2010. *Ordering Power: Contentious Politics and Authoritarian Leviathans in Southeast Asia*. New York: Cambridge University Press.

Slater, Dan, and Sofia Fenner. 2011. "State Power and Staying Power: Infrastructural Mechanisms and Authoritarian Durability." *Journal of International Affairs* 65:15–29.

Slater, Dan, Benjamin Smith, and Gautam Nair. 2014. "Economic Origins of Democratic Breakdown? The Redistributive Model and the Postcolonial State." *Perspectives on Politics* 12 (2):353–374.

Slemrod, Joe. 2019. "Tax Compliance and Enforcement." *Journal of Economic Literature* 57 (4):904–954.

Song, Zheng, and Wei Xiong. 2018. "Risks in China's Financial System." *Annual Review of Financial Economics* 10:261–286.

Stasavage, David. 2016. "Representation and Consent: Why They Arose in Europe and Not Elsewhere." *Annual Review of Political Science* 19 (1):145–162.

Steinmo, Sven. 1993. *Taxation and Democracy: Swedish, British, and American Approaches to Financing the Modern State*. New Haven, CT: Yale University Press.

Swank, Duane. 1998. "Funding the Welfare State: Globalization and the Taxation of Business in Advanced Market Economies." *Political Studies* 46 (4):671–692.

Takeuchi, Hiroki. 2014. *Tax Reform in Rural China: Revenue, Resistance, and Authoritarian Rule*. Cambridge: Cambridge University Press.

Tang, Wenfang. 2016. *Populist Authoritarianism: Chinese Political Culture and Regime Sustainability*. New York: Oxford University Press.

Tanner, Murray Scot. 1995. "How a Bill Becomes a Law in China: Stages and Processes in Lawmaking." *The China Quarterly* 141:39–64.

Tao Ran, Liu Mingxing, and Zhang Qi. 2003. "农民负担、政府管制与财政体制改革 [Peasants' Burden, Government Regulation and the Reform of the Fiscal System]." 经济研究[*Economic Research Journal*] 2003 (4):3–12.

Thaxton, Ralph. 2016. *Force and Contention in Contemporary China: Memory and Resistance in the Long Shadow of the Catastrophic Past*. New York: Cambridge University Press.

Tian, Yi, and Xu Zhao. 2008. 他乡之税 *[The Taxes from Another Town]*. Beijing: China CITIC Press.

Timmons, Jeffrey F. 2010. "Taxation and Representation in Recent History." *The Journal of Politics* 72 (1):191–208.

Tong, Yanqi, and Shaohua Lei. 2010. Large-Scale Mass Incidents and Government Responses in China. *International Journal of China Studies* 1 (2):487–508.

Trivedi, Viswanath U., Mohamed Shehata, and Stuart Mestelman. 2005. "Attitudes, Incentives, and Tax Compliance." *Canadian Tax Journal* 52, 29–61.

Truex, Rory. 2014. "The Returns to Office in a 'Rubber Stamp' Parliament." *American Political Science Review* 108 (2):235–251.

2016. *Making Autocracy Work: Representation and Responsiveness in Modern China*. New York: Cambridge University Press.

Tsai, Kellee S. 2007. *Capitalism without Democracy: The Private Sector in Contemporary China*. Ithaca, NY: Cornell University Press.

Tsebelis, George. 2002. *Veto Players: How Political Institutions Work*. Princeton, NJ: Princeton University Press.

Vogel, Ezra F. 2011. *Deng Xiaoping and the Transformation of China*. Cambridge, MA: Belknap Press of Harvard University Press.

Wallerstein, Michael, and Adam Przeworski. 1995. "Capital Taxation with Open Borders." *Review of International Political Economy* 2 (3):425–445.

Wang, Shaoguang, and Angang Hu. 1993. 中国国家能力报告 *[Report of Chinese State Capacity]*. Shenyang: Liaoning People's Press.

Wang, Xiaxin, and Yan Shen. 2014. "The Effect of China's Agricultural Tax Abolition on Rural Families' Incomes and Production." *China Economic Review* 29:185–199.

Wang, Yuhua. 2022. *The Rise and Fall of Imperial China: The Social Origins of State Development*. Princeton, NJ: Princeton University Press.

Whiting, Susan H. 2001. *Power and Wealth in Rural China: The Political Economy of Institutional Change*. New York: Cambridge University Press.

2004. "The Cadre Evaluation System at the Grass Roots: The Paradox of Party Rule." In *Holding China Together: Diversity and National Integration in the Post-Deng Era*, ed. Barry Naughton, and Dali Yang. New York: Cambridge University Press, 101–119.

2011. "Values in Land: Fiscal Pressures, Land Disputes, and Justice Claims in Rural and Peri-Urban China." *Urban Studies* 48 (3):569–587.

Whyte, Martin King. 2010. *Myth of the Social Volcano: Perceptions of Inequality and Distributive Injustice in Contemporary China*. Stanford, CA: Stanford University Press.

Wiens, David, Paul Poast, and William Roberts Clark. 2014. "The Political Resource Curse: An Empirical Re-evaluation." *Political Research Quarterly* 67 (4):783–794.

Winters, Jeffrey A. 2011. *Oligarchy*. New York: Cambridge University Press.

Wong, Christine. 1991. "Central–Local Relations in an Era of Fiscal Decline: The Paradox of Fiscal Decentralization in Post-Mao China." *The China Quarterly* 128:691–715.

2018. "An Update on Fiscal Reform." In *China's 40 Years of Reform and Development: 1978–2018*, ed. Ross Garnaut, Ligang Song, and Cai Fang Canberra: ANU Press, 271–290.

Wong, Christine, and Richard Bird. 2008. "Fiscal System in China: A Work in Progress." In *China's Great Economic Transformation*, ed. Loren Brandt and Thomas G. Rawski. Cambridge: Cambridge University Press, 429–466.

Wu, Jinglian. 2018. 中国经济改革进程 *[China's Economic Reform in Progress]*. Beijing: Zhongguo Dabaike Quanshu Press.

Wu, Yi. 2007. 小镇喧嚣: 一个乡镇政治运作的演绎与阐释 *[Noises in a Small Township: The Evolution and Interpretation of Political Processes in an Agricultural Township]*. Beijing: Sanlian Shudian.

Xiao, Tangbiao. 2005. "从农民心态看农村政治稳定状况–一个分析框架及其应用 [Peasants' Psychology and Rural Political Stability In China – A Framework and Its Application]." 华中师范大学学报(人文社会科学版)*[Journal of Huazhong Normal University(HUMANITIES AND SOCIAL SCIENCES)]* 44 (5):10–17.

Xie, Yu, and Xiang Zhou. 2014. "Income Inequality in Today's China." *Proceedings of the National Academy of Sciences (PNAS)* 111:6928–6933.

Xu, Chenggang. 2011. "The Fundamental Institutions of China's Reforms and Development." *Journal of Economic Literature* 49 (4):1076–1151.

Xu, Jianwei, Guangrong Ma, and Shi Li. 2013. "个人所得税改善中国收入分配了吗——基于对 1997—2011 年微观数据的动态评估 [Has the Personal Income Tax Improved China's Income Distribution? A Dynamic Assessment of the 1997–2011 Micro Data]." 中国社会科学 *[Chinese Social Science]* 6:53–71.

Xu, Jing and Ximing Yue. 2013. "Redistributive Impacts of the Personal Income Tax in Urban China." In Rising Inequality in China: Challenges to a Harmonious Society, eds. Shi Li, Hiroshi Sato, and Terry Sicular. Cambridge: Cambridge University Press. chapter, 362–383.

Yang, Dali. 2004. *Remaking the Chinese Leviathan: Market Transition and the Politics of Governance in China*. Stanford, California: Stanford University Press.

Yan, Hua, Taibiao Xia, and Jiandong Chen. 2016 "个人所得税收入流失率抽样调查." [Research on Personal Income Tax Evasion Based on Survey Sampling]. 税务研究 [Taxation Research] 11:48–52.

Yang, Wenhui, and Xiaoxiao Shen. 2021. "Can Social Welfare Buy Mass Loyalty?" *Governance* 34 (4):1213–1233.

Yang, Zhiyong. 2020. 新中国财政政策 70 年 *[China's Fiscal Policies in the Last Seventy Years]*. Beijing: Zhongguo caizheng jingji chubanshe.

Yao, Yang, and Muyang Zhang. 2015. "Subnational Leaders and Economic Growth: Evidence from Chinese Cities." *Journal of Economic Growth* 20 (4):405–436.

Zhan, Peng, Shi Li, and Xiaojing Xu. 2019. "Personal Income Tax Reform in China in 2018 and Its Impact on Income Distribution." *China & World Economy* 27 (3):25–48.

Zhang, Bin, and Moru Yang. 新中国财政收入70年 [*China's Fiscal Revenue in the Last Seventy Years*]. Beijing: Zhongguo caizheng jingji chubanshe.

Zhang, Changdong. 2019. "Asymmetric Mutual Dependence between State and Capitalists in China." *Politics and Society* 47 (2):149–176.

2021. *Governing and Ruling: The Political Logic of Taxation in China*. Ann Arbor: University of Michigan Press.

Zhang, Changdong, and Bruce Dickson. 2024. "The Art of Plucking the Goose: Chinese Urban Residents' Tax Consciousness." *Governance* 37 (2):375–393.

Zhang, Shuguang. 1996. "国家能力与制度变革和社会转型 [State Capacity and Institutional Change and Social Transformation]." In 张曙光经济学书评集 [*Collection of Zhang Shuguang's Economic Book Reviews*]. Beijing: China Finance and Economic Press, 138–159.

Zhang, Taisu. 2022. *The Ideological Foundations of Qing Taxation: Belief Systems, Politics, and Institutions*. Cambridge: Cambridge University Press.

Zhang, Xuebo. 2018. 中国税收立法四十年 [*Forty Years of Tax Legislation in China*]. Beijing: People's Publishing House.

Zhao, Dingxin. 2009. "The Mandate of Heaven and Performance Legitimation in Historical and Contemporary China." *American Behavioral Scientist* 53 (3):416–433.

Zhou, Feizhou. 2012. 以利为利 [*Take Interest as Interest: Fiscal Relationship and Local Government Behavior*]. Shanghai: Sanlian Press.

Zhu, Qing. 2014. "完善我国地方税体系的构想 [Conceptions of the Improvement of China's Sub-National Tax System]." 财贸经济 [*Finance & Trade Economics*] 2014 (5):5–13.

Acknowledgment

The authors are listed in alphabetical order and contributed equally to this work. This research was supported by University of Texas at Austin and the Institute of Public Governance, Peking University. We thank Ning Li, Shengqiao Lin, and Kenny (Ling) Miao for their excellent research assistance. We are gratefully to two anonymous reviewers and the editor, Qi Zhang, for their insightful comments and suggestions.

Cambridge Elements

Chinese Economy and Governance

Luke Qi Zhang
Fudan University

Luke Qi Zhang is Associate Professor at the China Center for Economic Studies of the School of Economics at Fudan University. He specializes in the political economy of authoritarianism generally and how elite politics affects policy making and economic outcomes in China specifically. His book (co-authored with Mingxing Liu) *Revolutionary Legacy, Power Structure, and Grassroots Capitalism under the Red Flag in China* (Cambridge University Press, 2019) proposes a theory of localized property rights protection under authoritarianism, and applies the theory to the private sector development in both the Mao era and the current reform era in China.

Mingxing Liu
Peking University

Mingxing Liu is Professor of the China Institute for Educational Finance Research at Peking University. He works on China's elite politics, economic growth, and local governance. He has published numerous academic articles in international and Chinese journals such as the *American Political Science Review, Comparative Political Studies, Comparative Politics*, and *Journal of Politics*.

Daniel Mattingly
Yale University

Daniel Mattingly is Associate Professor in the Department of Political Science at Yale University. He studies the domestic and international politics of authoritarian regimes, with a focus on China. His book *The Art of Political Control in China* (Cambridge University Press, 2020) received the Best Book Award from the Democracy and Autocracy Section of the American Political Science Association and was named a best book of the year by *Foreign Affairs*.

Editorial Advisory Board

Hanming Fang, *School of Economics, University of Pennsylvania*
Jean Hong, *Department of Political Science, University of Michigan*
Roselyn Hsueh, *Department of Political Science, Temple University*
Margaret Pearson, *Department of Government and Politics, University of Maryland, College Park*
Meg Rithmire, *Harvard Business School*
Victor Shih, *School of Global Policy and Strategy, UC San Diego*
Kellee Tsai, *Division of Social Sciences, Hongkong University of Science & Technology*
Colin Lixin Xu, *Senior Economist, the World Bank*
Jun Zhang, *Dean of School of Economics, Fudan University*

About the Series

The works in this Elements series examine China's economy, governance, and policy-making process. Members of the political and business communities will find the series a valuable guide to navigate China's complex policy and governance system and understand its business environment.

Cambridge Elements⁼

Chinese Economy and Governance

Elements in the Series

Meritocracy or Patronage? Political Foundations of China's Economic Transition
Fubing Su and Ran Tao

Elite Conflicts and the Path to Economic Decentralization
Dong Zhang, Mingxing Liu and Victor Shih

Taxation and Governance in Contemporary China
Xiaobo Lü and Changdong Zhang

A full series listing is available at: www.cambridge.org/ECEG

Printed by Integrated Books International,
United States of America